Finding the Lone Woman
of
San Nicolas Island

Based on a True Story

By R.C. Nidever

STANSBURY
PUBLISHING
Chico, Ca.

Finding the Lone Woman of San Nicolas Island
Copyright © 2017 by R.C. Nidever

ISBN: 978-1-935807-26-1 paperback
978-1-935807-27-8 Kindle
978-1-935807-28-5 ePub

Library of Congress Control Number: 2017933608

Cover design by Connie Ballou, Back Alley Graphics

Stansbury Publishing is an imprint of
Heidelberg Graphics

All rights reserved. No part of this book may be be reproduced or transmitted in any form or by any means, electronic or mechanical, including photocopying, recording, or by any information storage and retrieval system without permission in writing from the copyright holders or publisher, except for reviews.

To the memory of

the original inhabitants

of the California Channel Islands

"… here was an undoubted testimony that there was scarce any condition in the world so miserable but there was something negative or something positive to be thankful for in it; and let this stand as a direction from the experience of the most miserable of all conditions in this world, that we may always find in it something to comfort ourselves from and to set in the description of good and evil on the credit side of the account."

—Robinson Crusoe

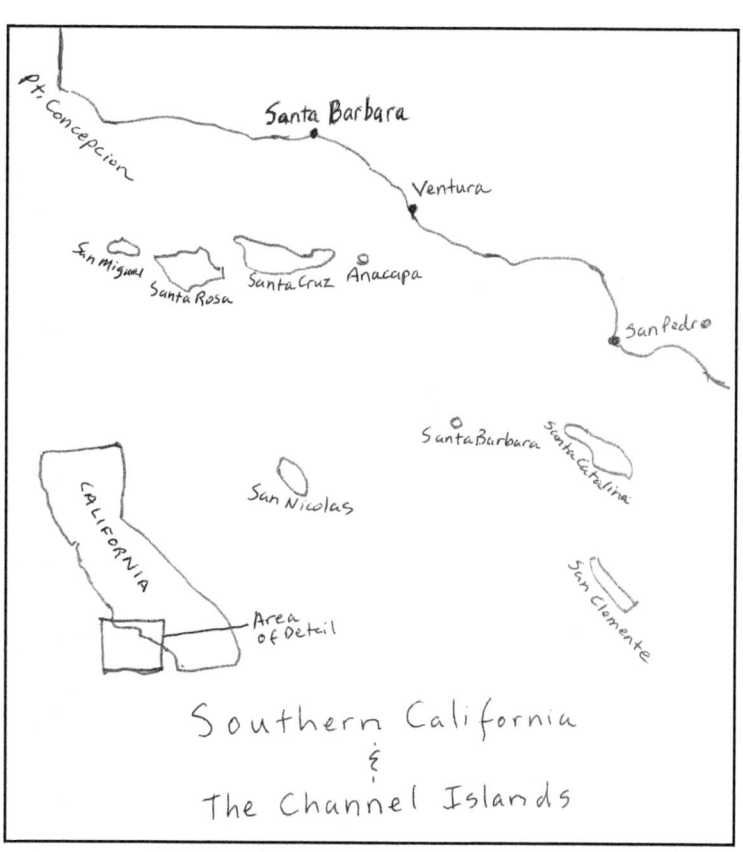

Chapter One

The Perspective of an Old Pioneer

Santa Barbara, California
April 1883

Most folks who have been around as long as me—just passed my eighty-first birthday—love to gripe and grumble about how miserable it is being so damn old. You probably know one yourself—some old fogey who can't talk about anything but aches and pains and not being long for this world.

But me, I'm not like that at all. I don't ever complain about old age, or anything else. I learned years ago that it's about as worthwhile as blasting a shotgun at the sky because you don't like the weather.

So why am I this way? Well, for one, I suppose I did enough complaining in my younger days for a whole lifetime, even one as long as mine. Not to mention that I expressed many of my complaints through the barrel of a gun.

But there is another reason, one that is harder to explain. You'll have to hear the story I'm about to tell to really understand it. For now, I'll just say that somebody once showed me there's really no good reason at all to complain about anything. Even old age.

Hell, there's even one thing about being old I actually like. Let's see, how can I put it? The word that comes to mind is "perspective." Old age, at least in my case, has brought a sharper perspective of the moments in life that for better or worse made me who I am.

I suppose in this way life is a bit like climbing a mountain. In our younger days all we care about is moving upwards, and never stop to look back at the places or people left behind. But as the years pass we gradually gain a better view of where we've been. The further up you climb, the better you can see the path that got you there, and also other paths that may have made the climb a little easier.

At my age, the climbing is done. I'm now content to just sit and take in the view with my eighty-one years of perspective. Fortunately, I've got a lot to look back on—a childhood on the frontier, years of hunting buffalo, trapping beaver and fighting Indians in the Rocky Mountains, my voyage west to California and Santa Barbara, sailing the Channel Islands, raising a family with a beautiful Mexican wife—more than my share, I would say, of thrilling incidents and unforgettable days.

However, the older I get, there is one day which stands out much more than any other—April 10, 1835, which happened to be my thirty-third birthday. It was a day that began like any other, but by the time it ended I was a different person, for reasons that had nothing to do with being another year older.

Three notable things happened that day—

For a few terrifying moments, I was sure I was about to die.

I began to learn not to complain so much.

An Indian woman got left behind on San Nicolas Island.

THE PERSPECTIVE OF AN OLD PIONEER

April 10, 1835, came shortly after I first arrived here in Santa Barbara. On that day I was on board a small schooner called the *Peor es Nada*. The captain was my friend Isaac Sparks, and the crew was me and two Chumash Indians from the Santa Barbara Mission.

We'd been hired by Father Ramirez of the San Gabriel Mission in Los Angeles. He had just heard some surprising news—there were still some Indians out on the island called San Nicolas. However, they were on the verge of dying out, as they already had on the other islands in that area.

It looked to be a quick, simple job—sail out to San Nicolas, locate the few Indians still there, get them loaded onto the ship (we'd been assured they would go peacefully) and deliver them to the mission.

It was a job I thought I'd enjoy because back in those days I hated Indians—for reasons I'll explain later—and so I was happy to help make San Nicolas Island one more place in the world where they no longer existed.

But then something unexpected took place. Something that changed the way I see the world, and everyone in it. Especially Indians. Funny thing is, it would've never happened without the fateful timing of some really foul weather.

There's no telling how different my view of things might be if that heavy gale hadn't hit us as we arrived at San Nicolas Island. It was the gale that forced us to leave the island while there was still someone on it, and caused me to stumble and fall overboard into a turbulent sea.

I was just seconds away from drowning when someone suddenly grabbed me from behind and pulled me upwards. Before I knew it I was back on board and hanging over the stern rail, spewing seawater and gasping for air. It all happened so quickly I wasn't even sure who had just saved my life.

The other three—Sparks and the two Indians—scurried about as the ship sailed away through huge swells and the howling wind. As I struggled to regain my breath, I looked back at the island and saw the woman who for some reason went missing as we were loading the others onto the ship. She stood on a large plateau just below the main ridge of the island, and was waving her arms. In one hand she held what appeared to be a spear or a long stick. Coming up a trail just below her was a pack of dogs.

I turned around to see if anyone else had noticed her. At the same time I realized that because the gale was blowing from the west, we could not turn the ship around and go back. We had no choice but to run before the wind, which was blowing us away from the island. And then, at that moment, I became aware of two things.

One, I felt sympathy for the woman on the island. This was a strange and new experience for me—feeling sorry for an Indian.

Two, someone was looking back to check on me, and make sure I'd regained my breath. It was Pedro, a Chumash Indian, and his clothes, like mine, were dripping wet.

As I realized it was an Indian who'd just saved me from drowning, I turned back around and looked at the island, but could no longer see the woman or the dogs.

Well, as I said, old age brings a sharper perspective to such moments. Many years passed before I really began to understand the impact of what happened out at San Nicolas Island on April 10, 1835. But now I can clearly see how that day changed my life, and also the lives of many others, in ways none of us will ever forget.

Like any story worth telling, there is much more to this one than just the story itself. To merely tell you the bare details of what happened to an Indian woman on a distant island would still make for an intriguing narrative, but wouldn't show how this story changed lives, and how it sums up the fate of Indians in this country.

So, to really tell the story of the Lone Woman of San Nicolas Island, I will also tell you about the lives of those who were around when it happened, and the times we lived in. Otherwise, this story would be conspicuously incomplete, like a portrait with half the face left blank.

I'll begin by telling you about my own life, and how I changed from being a man who killed Indians to one who instead learned from them.

If you had known me in my younger days, you'd probably think I'd be the last person in the world to end up telling such a story. But here I am, and here's how it came to be.

My name is George Nidever. My odd last name (pronounced with a long "i" by the way) originates from my grandfather, who came to this country from Germany in 1760. His name was Johann Marcus Niedhoffer, but his three sons, in typical American fashion, decided to simplify things, hence the unique surname.

I was born in 1802 in Sullivan County, Tennessee. My father was a farmer and also an excellent hunter. My mother, a schoolteacher, made sure her nine children could all read and write. While growing up I was never too keen on farming or schoolwork, but I sure did take to hunting.

From the moment I was big enough to hold a rifle, it was all I wanted to do.

By the age of twelve, I was a better shot than anyone I knew, and won every shooting contest around. This gave me the feeling I was someone special. I thought of myself as a man long before actually becoming one. I was as cocksure as they come, and didn't give a whit about what anyone else thought of me.

If I can say one thing in my defense, it's this: when it comes to hunting, in my day I had few equals. And when a person is that good at something, it's hard not to be a little big-headed.

Also, I grew up on the frontier. My father explained to me at a young age what I needed to do to survive.

"Whether you're farming or hunting," he said, "you better know how to defend yourself. It's likely that someday you'll have to kill someone to avoid getting killed by them.

"You especially have to watch out," he always warned me, "for the god-damned Indians."

As I learned while growing up, there was a lot of bad blood between Indians and folks like us who were settling the frontier. As Americans started moving west, we claimed land for ourselves that had always belonged to Indians.

As more of us came, conflicts arose over who would control the land. I don't think anyone realized it at the time, but this was the beginning of a long war between Indians and whites—a war that spread through America and continues to this day.

I guess it couldn't be avoided. Whenever two very different types of people lay claim to the same land, there will be a war.

So, from a very early age, I saw Indians as the enemy.

And because they were so different from us, I believed they were somehow not really human beings. I had no guilt or hesitation to kill them.

In 1820, my family moved to Fort Smith, Arkansas. On the way there, I killed my first Indian, which made me feel very proud. It was like the feeling I had when I dropped my first deer.

It happened while we were passing through country inhabited by the Osage Indians. We always kept a watch at night, and one night when it was my turn I heard some suspicious sounds coming from where our horses were picketed. I quietly approached that area and saw two Indians trying to steal our horses. I quickly aimed my rifle and fired at the closer of the two, and hit him square in the chest. The other one ran away before I could get another shot off.

I went over to calm down the horses and check that the Indian was dead. I kicked his body with my foot until I was sure of it. My father and older brother John ran over and, seeing what had happened, slapped me on the back.

"Nice shot, George," said John. "That's one Indian who sure as hell won't be stealing any more horses."

In the year 1828 I organized a party of about twenty men from the Fort Smith area that left for the Rocky Mountains to trap beaver and hunt buffalo. Included were my two hunting partners—Alex Sinclair, whose sister was married to my brother Jacob, and my brother Mark, who was about a year younger than me. The three of us often hunted together, and there was no one I liked and trusted more than Alex and Mark.

For the next five years our party did quite well. We

trapped and hunted in various parts of the Rockies, and traded our skins in San Fernando de Taos, in the region known as New Mexico. There we met some Mexican trappers who joined our party, and from them I learned to speak Spanish.

I gradually earned a reputation as one of the best hunters around. I *never* missed. I won many bets on who could kill the most buffalo. Eventually such wagers stopped, as I could no longer get anyone to bet against me. Mark and Alex used to joke that I could kill anything even if I only had a corncob.

It was a great life. I was admired and successful. I feared or looked up to no one. Other hunters and trappers said of me "he has the hair of the bear," which was the highest praise a mountain man could receive.

However, my life in those days was far from perfect, due to one thing—the presence of so many Indians. We could never relax in Indian country—which was just about everywhere. Various tribes were often following us and trying to steal, sometimes successfully, our horses, furs or supplies. Others threatened to attack us if we didn't agree to trade some of our valuable possessions for their worthless ones.

If it wasn't the Comanche, it was the Arapahoe. If not them, it was the Pawnee, the Sioux, the Crow, the Blackfeet, or the Ree. At the time, it never occurred to me that Indians had any more right to the land than we did. I didn't care who was there first. All that mattered to me is who would be there in the end.

During the first five years or so, we had many run-ins with Indians but never lost a single man. This was because our party didn't hesitate to show the Indians we were not afraid to fight and kill them.

A good example of this was our first encounter with the Comanche. A group of six from our party, including me, was out hunting buffalo one day a mile or so from camp. Suddenly a war party of about forty mounted Comanche came out from the timber, and shot a number of arrows at us. We high-tailed it back to camp, where the rest of our party grabbed their rifles and formed a defensive line.

The Comanche pulled up and decided not to attack us, but one of them, more daring than the rest, charged toward us. He came close enough to throw his lance, which we easily dodged. We assumed he would ride away from us in a side-to-side motion, and, as shots are always uncertain when fired at someone riding in such a way, we would've let him pass, but instead of doing this he rode off from our party in a perfectly straight line. Loath to lose such a chance, I drew a bead on him and tumbled him out of his saddle. Two of our men caught his horse. This brought forth a yell from the Indians, but they did not trouble us anymore.

Protecting ourselves from possible Indian attacks also required vigilance and caution. Of the mountain men I knew who got killed by Indians, most died because they were careless in their habits. Our party, for example, always kept a night watch of at least four men. Many times this prevented an attack that would've been the end of us.

Despite taking such precautions, in the spring of 1833 Indians murdered two members of our party. For me, this began a personal vendetta that didn't end until that fateful day of April 10, 1835.

Our party had just arrived at the north fork of the Arkansas River, which looked to be plentiful with beaver. However, we were short on meat and also feed for our animals, so six of us set out to search the surrounding country.

The six were my brother Mark and I and four others—Crist, Basey, Dye and Graham. After a few hours we found a valley with a herd of buffalo and plenty of feed. Four of us stayed to get buffalo. Mark and Crist volunteered to go back and lead the rest of the party to our location.

We had seen no sign of Indians in this area, but for some reason, about two hours after Mark and Crist left, I got a feeling they were around. Not long after that, sure enough a group of about twenty Arapahoe warriors rode into the valley and, noticing us, began whooping and hollering and riding in our direction. The four of us were forced to take cover, abandoning a large amount of freshly killed buffalo meat we had hanging up. The Arapahoes took our meat and rode off.

After they left, we decided to head back to the rest of the party and make sure everyone was all right. About a mile or so from their location, we rounded the corner of a small hill and came upon the dead bodies of Crist and my brother Mark. They had been ambushed by Indians, then stabbed to death and scalped.

It's hard for me to describe how I felt. Both sadness and rage. Mark was my brother, and a good man in the prime of life. He and Alex had been my closest companions for years.

As we buried him, I began to burn with a desire for revenge. I wanted to find the nearest Indians and kill them, and keep on killing them until there were no more left.

At the time, it never occurred to me that an Indian might feel the same as I did about a murdered brother.

I was angry and hell-bent on revenge. But I wasn't stupid, and I didn't want to sacrifice my life, or the lives of the other men in my party, to get my revenge. I decided to just bide my time and wait for the right opportunity. I knew it would eventually come, and it did, but not without more tragedy for me and my party.

Every summer during those years, a trappers' rendezvous took place. That year, 1833, it was at Pierre's Hole, Wyoming. Our party always attended this rendezvous. It was a good place to get supplies for the coming year, find out which areas were trapped out, and whether any Indian tribes were on the warpath.

About the beginning of August, the various parties of trappers began to leave the rendezvous for their respective hunting grounds. We left in the company of two other parties led by Frapp and Wyatt, as our course would be the same for some distance. Our first camp was about fifteen miles from Pierre's Hole. Frapp's and Wyatt's men camped together, and we were just a short distance behind them.

The next morning we packed up and rode ahead to their camp, and upon arriving saw about a hundred Indians riding toward us. We immediately recognized them as Blackfeet, known to be the most dangerous tribe in that region. They had discovered us before we saw them and decided to attack us.

We quickly formed a breastwork with our packs and dispatched a rider on our fleetest horse back to Pierre's Hole to get reinforcements.

As soon as the Indians came within range they began firing, to which we replied. Fortunately, we managed to hold them off until about fifty men from Pierre's Hole arrived. When the Indians saw this they retreated and took cover in a narrow belt of woods alongside a river.

We formed a long line of attack and surrounded the woods, slowly trapping the Indians against the river. Several of our men were shot but none fatally. The Indians, however, were dropping left and right. After a few hours they began trying to escape by jumping in the river and swimming to the other side.

Just as the fighting appeared to be dying down, I saw my friend Alex Sinclair fall to the ground and press both hands to his stomach. There was blood oozing out between his fingers. He had taken a bullet and I arrived at his side just in time to see him take his last breath.

The Indians had taken away the two people I was closest to. When Mark was killed, at least I still had Alex. But with both of them dead and gone, I suddenly felt very much alone.

It gave me little satisfaction that we killed over twenty Indians. My thirst for revenge had just become even stronger.

In April of the following year, we were trapping along the north fork of the Platte River. We had a camp set up with our horses picketed about a hundred yards away. One morning I went to bring in the horses with a member of our party named Gillum when suddenly a band of about eighty Ree Indians rode down upon us. I barely escaped back to camp but Gillum was not so lucky. The Ree killed him and stole all of our horses.

This incident forced us to travel three hundred miles on foot to the Green River Valley, the site of that year's rendezvous. I arrived there wondering how much longer I wanted to hunt and trap for a living. The Indians were a frequent source of trouble and had killed my brother and best friend. Was I next?

I also knew that the buffalo and beaver were getting hunted out. Over the years, the number of hunters and trappers had steadily increased. Game was getting scarce and the competition fierce. I wasn't sure what I would do next, but then my reputation as a hunter brought an unexpected opportunity.

At the rendezvous that year I met a well-known explorer, Captain Joseph Walker. He was preparing to depart in search of a new route through the Sierra Nevada into California, and asked me to join him. I would be in charge of keeping the party supplied with meat. This meant I'd be working for someone else for the first time in my life, but I knew it was an opportunity I couldn't pass up.

The chance to go further west appealed to my appetite for adventure. At the time, California was still over ten years away from becoming a part of the United States, and not many Americans had been there. It was still part of Mexico then, and before that belonged to Spain.

Also, during those years in the Rockies, I occasionally heard stories from some of my Mexican compañeros about California. They described it as a peaceful land of oceanside pueblos, mild winters, plentiful game, and beautiful señoritas.

The Walker party, totaling thirty-six men, set out for the Sierra Nevada in July of 1834. We passed by Salt Lake and from there went south, intending to trap a little on the Marys River before heading west. The Indians, however, made this impossible. First they stole our traps, and then came to us and demanded our horses in exchange for letting us pass through their country.

We refused to meet such a demand and from then on

the Indians stayed very close by. They were no doubt waiting for an opportunity to attack us. In response we doubled our guard and proceeded on with the greatest of caution.

Just before reaching the Sierra Nevada, our trail led us into a large, thick stand of willows. Realizing it would be a perfect place for an ambush, we detoured around it through the adjoining plain. Just a few minutes after leaving the trail, we found that taking such a precaution was wise, as about two hundred Indians emerged from the willows. Staying on that trail would've made dead men of us all.

The Indians then separated into several distinct bodies or companies, probably representing the respective villages to which they belonged. We halted and prepared for a fight.

About thirty-five Indians advanced toward us. We allowed them to get quite close before unleashing a barrage of fire which immediately killed more than half of them. This completely threw the Indians into disarray. They retreated and after that no longer bothered us.

I found one more chance for revenge before arriving in California. Just after reaching the Sierra Nevada, I went ahead of the group one day in search of water and a camping place. I entered a heavily timbered area where I noticed some fresh tracks. Looking back in the direction I'd come from, I saw two Indians. They were trotting along the same trail I was on. I thought they were following my tracks, so I lost no time in getting off the trail and finding a big tree to hide behind.

It took them a few minutes to reach me, as they stopped every few yards and looked back as if being pursued. As they passed within a few feet of me, I could tell they had not seen me, or my tracks. At first I had a notion to let them go, but then the deaths of my brother and best friend came to mind. It didn't matter to me that they were from a different tribe than the Indians who killed Mark and Alex. They were all the same to me.

The Indians were traveling in single file. I waited until they passed me and were in a straight line from my position. Then I stepped out from behind the tree and dropped both of them with a single shot. I took their blankets, the only articles they had worth taking, as they were armed only with bows.

By this time I'd killed a lot of Indians. I suppose I should've felt satisfied that I'd avenged the deaths of Mark and Alex. But I didn't. Upon arriving in California, I was still of a mind to kill Indians whenever possible. I thought I'd never be able to forget what they had taken from me.

However, the day of April 10, 1835, was fast approaching.

Chapter Two

A Different World

We came down out of the Sierra Nevada and into California in October 1834, through a pass later named after Captain Walker. We were the first Americans, I believe, to explore the area in between the Merced River and Tuolumne River, and the valley now called Yosemite. From there we continued on into the San Joaquin Valley, which occupies most of the central part of California.

It didn't take long to notice the differences between California and every other place I'd been. Back then it was still a part of Mexico, and everyone spoke Spanish. I was considered a foreigner, and there were very few Americans. But the biggest difference of all was the condition of the Indians.

I saw the first indication of this while still in the foothills of the Sierra Nevada. The Walker party happened to cross paths with a group of vigilantes. They were from the San Jose area and pursuing of a band of Indians who had stolen fifty horses from their ranch. They asked if we wanted to join their group, in return for some of the horses if caught. Four members of our party, including me, decided to do so.

The next day we located the Indians' camp, but it was mostly deserted. There were just a few old squaws and several young children remaining there. Something about the camp immediately caught my eye—obvious signs of butchered horses.

"Why would they do such a thing?" I asked, but no one responded to my question. Instead, the vigilantes did something that shocked those of us from the Walker party—they opened fire on the defenseless old squaws and children, and gunned down every last one of them.

Right then I wondered what was going on. The butchering of the horses meant they'd been stolen for food, which indicated that the Indians were unable to feed themselves through the usual ways—hunting, fishing, collecting acorns and berries and the like.

I'd also never seen anyone gun down women and children like that. Yes, I hated Indians, but was appalled by what the vigilantes had done.

A few days later I saw something similar. I was hunting with a few other members of the Walker party near the Stanislaus River when we heard rifle shots coming from just to the north of us.

After hiking up river for a few minutes, during which time we heard more shooting, we rounded a bend and saw a dozen or so Indians lined up on their knees, surrounded by about thirty Mexican soldiers. A Franciscan Catholic priest was also there. Some five or six Indians lay dead on the ground.

We quickly took cover before anyone saw us. The other men decided they wanted no part of this scene, and quietly retreated back down river. However, I wanted to stay and see what was going on, so I hid in the brush and motioned to the others to go on.

I soon realized I was witnessing an execution. What I

couldn't understand, though, was why, before each Indian was shot he was first baptized by the Franciscan priest.

Again, I wondered what on earth was going on. Why were apparently defenseless Indians being shot down in such a way? And why was the holy sacrament of baptism a part of this?

A few days later I began to get some answers to these questions. Thinking about it now, I realize that the story of the Lone Woman of San Nicolas Island didn't really start on April 10, 1835. Actually, it begins way back in 1770, when a Franciscan missionary named Junipero Serra first arrived in California.

About this time I met an American named George Yount, who had been in California for several years. It was Yount who first explained to me what had happened to Indians in California during the sixty or so years of Spanish and Mexican rule.

"From what I've heard, it all began with the best of intentions," Yount told me. "Apparently, Father Serra truly believed the Catholic Church of Spain could save the souls of all those Indians, and provide them a better life.

"Whether he saved any souls, I can't say. But the missions he built ended up wiping out many Indian tribes. If Serra were alive today—he died back in 1785—I think he'd find it difficult to explain how spreading the word of God could cause such an outcome."

From Yount, and later from others, I learned a lot about the period of California history now called the mission era, which ended about a decade before I arrived here.

During the eighteenth century, Spain spread its overseas empire by building Catholic missions, protected by a military force. Junipero Serra was head of the missions in Mexico, and once those were established, Spain sent him north, into the area the Spanish named California.

Serra, and the other padres who followed him here, apparently couldn't see that Indians have the same desire all human beings share—to decide for themselves how to live.

Perhaps even worse, the Spaniards also brought to California diseases such as measles, smallpox, and malaria, which were very deadly to the Indians. It didn't take long for these diseases to spread among the natives, killing many of them and sometimes wiping out whole villages.

Over the next thirty years or so, the Franciscans built about twenty missions along the coast of California. The Spaniards also built military forts, called presidios, to ensure the Indian converts could always be kept in line.

When the missionaries and their military escorts came to California, they encountered mostly peaceful Indian tribes that had no history of contact with the white man. There was apparently little resistance to the building of the missions and the presidios. Gradually, thousands of Indians left their villages to live at the missions and become converted Catholics, under the supervision of the mission padres.

I don't know how the padres converted so many Indians. Certainly, many gifts were given, and promises made of a richer life. Also, in those first years, Serra, the other padres, and the soldiers of the presidios were careful not to use force or in any way treat the Indians badly.

The Indian tribe I know the most about is the one from this area, called the Chumash. Their experience during the mission era was similar to that of many other tribes in California.

The Chumash inhabited a large territory, spanning from Ventura up to San Luis Obispo. They also occupied some of the Channel Islands, a chain of eight islands off the coast of Santa Barbara and Los Angeles.

Records kept by the missionaries claim that by about 1795 almost all of the Chumash had converted to Catholicism, including one named Yanonali, who was the tribe's chief.

By then, the Santa Barbara mission complex included a large church and presidio, several chapels, a granary, a grist mill, a weaving mill, a tannery, a reservoir with irrigation canals, and about 250 adobe houses for the converts. Surrounding it all were hundreds of acres used for raising crops and livestock.

About this time the missions began to decline. In 1801 an outbreak of pneumonia and other diseases killed over eight hundred Indians. Soon after that came the first sign of rebellion. A young Chumash woman began speaking of a dream in which she saw her people abandon their Christian beliefs and return to worshipping their old gods.

Word of this dream spread throughout the area, and things were never the same after that. The Indians wanted more freedom, but the padres refused to allow it. The soldiers from the presidios began pursuing any convert who left the mission. If caught, the Indians were forcibly returned and often brutally punished, or even executed, which I saw happen that day by the Stanislaus River.

All in all, the Chumash came to miss their former way of life. In particular, I was told, they didn't like the strict rules regarding the separation of unmarried men and women.

Finally, in 1824, the Chumash revolted. It began at the Santa Ynez Mission, which was the next mission up the coast from Santa Barbara, and spread to the La Purisma Concepcion Mission, which was just north of Santa Ynez, and then down to Santa Barbara.

The rebels at Santa Ynez burned down the mission and took the padres hostage. Later that day, the Indians at La Purisma Concepcion also revolted.

The presidios sent about one hundred soldiers in response, but it took them almost a month to end the conflict, which resulted in the deaths of over twenty Indians and two soldiers. Seven rebels were executed and many others put in prison.

Here in Santa Barbara, the Indians heard of the revolts up north and decided to do the same. Armed with only bows and arrows and about a half-dozen stolen rifles, they took control of the mission complex and somehow kept the soldiers from taking it back. After nightfall, perhaps figuring they could not hold back the soldiers again the next day, most of the Indians chose to quietly leave the mission. They headed inland to the San Joaquin Valley to join fugitives from Santa Ynez and La Purisma Concepcion.

Imagine the reaction of the padres the next morning, when they found the mission mostly empty of Indians. Without them, the padres would have no reason to be there.

The next day about fifty soldiers set out in pursuit, accompanied by Father Sarria of the Santa Barbara Mission. Sarria believed the only way to get the Indians to return was by offering them a full pardon, better working conditions and more freedom. This strategy apparently worked, as about two-thirds of the Indians came back to the mission.

But soon, other events finally ended the mission era in

California. Around the same time as the Chumash revolt, Mexico gained its independence from Spain, and made two big changes here.

One was the awarding of land grants, which gave huge chunks of Chumash land to well-connected individuals to establish large ranchos.

The other was taking over control of the missions from the Franciscans. Almost all mission land, many thousands of acres, was given away. At the same time, the government declared all Indians free and able to move at will.

These changes brought even worse times for the Indians. They were promised a portion of the Mission lands, but it never happened. The government believed the new skills the Indians had learned at the missions would allow them to fit into Spanish-Mexican society. Instead they ended up mostly as slaves and bandits in what was once their land.

As the missions declined, some Indians attempted to go back to their old ways, but it was too late. Their land was now controlled by the rancheros and the Mexican government. Those who tried to return to the Chumash village way of life were driven off the land, especially when trying to hunt or fish.

Many ended up working on the ranchos, where they typically received just enough food, clothing and shelter to keep them alive. Most of the rancheros saw Indians as a lower type of human being and never tried to make them a part of Spanish society.

Some survived by stealing livestock and crops. Others left to join those who remained in the San Joaquin Valley after the 1824 revolt.

The Chumash, who'd lived here for probably thousands of years, were almost gone. The few hundred or so that remained were left with nothing. And it all happened in just about sixty years time.

Meanwhile, out on the Channel Islands a similar result took place. Six of the islands are quite large—the biggest one, Santa Cruz Island, is twenty-five miles in length and had several villages. The other large islands—San Miguel, Santa Rosa, Santa Catalina, San Clemente, and San Nicolas—also had one or more villages.

These islanders depended on trade and marriage with their coastal relatives. So as the mainland Chumash slowly dwindled away during the mission era, so did the island villages. When I arrived in Santa Barbara in early 1835, only one remained. It was on San Nicolas Island, which is seventy miles from the coast, some twenty-five to fifty miles further out than the other islands.

The Walker party left to explore more of the Sierra Nevada, but I decided to stay behind and join my new friend George Yount on a hunting expedition.

According to Yount, there was abundant game in California but not a lot of hunters. In particular, there was a big demand for what became known as "soft gold"—the skins of the sea otter. The coast of California was still thick with otter, and pelts sold for as much as twenty dollars each.

So we set off for San Francisco to do some hunting off its coast. On the way, I again saw something showing the dire circumstances of Indians in California.

One afternoon while setting up camp along the San Joaquin River, Yount noticed what appeared to be an abandoned Indian village just above us. While he prepared supper, I set out to have a look. Arriving at the huts, I looked into some of them, but found them empty. I walked around a bit and saw no sign of Indians.

At this point it was getting dark, so I started to head back to camp. Then I heard a loud moan, sounding like it came from a child, which I traced to one of the huts. Looking inside, I saw a small Indian girl, maybe five years old, seated in the far side of the hut. She tried to talk to me, but I could not understand her language. I left her and went back to inform Yount about what I'd seen.

I told him the child looked very weak and asked if we should rescue her. He refused, saying he feared the Indians might return and track the girl to our camp. That night we heard her crying out so in the morning we went to check her condition. We found her so weak she could not sit up. Upon bringing her out of the hut we saw she was quite thin, and obviously had not eaten for days.

We took her to our camp and gave her a piece of boiled meat. It was pitiful to see the eagerness with which she ate it up. We made some clothes for her, and with a little care she soon recovered. After finishing our hunting expedition, Yount took her with him to his rancho in the Napa Valley.

I asked Yount why he thought the little girl was abandoned. "I can't say for sure," he said. "I just hope she's too young to remember whatever did happen."

The hunting I did with Yount went well, but after a few days he departed for his rancho. This left me without a hunting partner, and also without a hunting license, which at the time were difficult for foreigners to obtain from the Mexican government.

However, as fate would have it, an American trading vessel had just arrived in San Francisco. It was about to return to the East Coast but on the way back planned to make a stop in Santa Barbara. Yount had heard the otter were thick in that area and recommended I book passage on the ship. He assured me I would have no problem getting a hunting license there, as the captain of the Santa Barbara Port was an American who Yount happened to know. He also wrote me a letter of introduction to take along.

Before I left, Yount told me he'd heard that another Yankee hunter he knew had recently arrived in Santa Barbara.

"I don't know if he's still there, but if he is you should definitely make his acquaintance. His name is Isaac Sparks, but everyone calls him Zack.

"Zack is a good hunter and an experienced sailor. The last I heard he was looking to charter a ship for hunting otter out on the islands down there. If he can make that happen, I'm sure he'd like to have someone like you along with him."

I didn't know it at the time, but I had just been introduced, so to speak, to the man who would become my hunting partner and close friend, and play a major role in the story of the Lone Woman of San Nicolas Island.

Chapter Three

Mission Indians, a Señorita, and a Ship

I can still clearly recall, after nearly fifty years, the voyage from San Francisco down to Santa Barbara. It was my first time on a ship, the sky was clear and the waters calm. I spent hours gazing at the vast expanse of the Pacific Ocean. The coastline revealed mile after mile of high sheer cliffs, half-circle coves, and white-sand beaches. I think I knew right then I'd never leave California.

Two beautiful sights appeared as the ship neared Santa Barbara. One was the Channel Islands. Four of the eight islands of this chain mark the southern boundary of the Santa Barbara Channel. Three of these four—Santa Cruz, San Miguel, and Santa Rosa—are so large and mountainous that even from a distance they look like giant green monsters rising out of the water.

To the eyes of a Tennessee-born mountain man, such a stunning scene of calm blue ocean and green islands seemed almost unreal. Upon first sight, I remember thinking that heaven was right here on earth, and I'd just found it.

The other sight to behold was the little pueblo of Santa Barbara. It's in a beautiful location, ringed in the front by white-sand beaches and in the back by dark green mountains, called the Santa Ynez. In between is a plain of about two miles, sloping slightly upwards, on which the town sits.

At the time I arrived, in early 1835, Santa Barbara was much smaller than it is today. There were just two roads, and the fifty or so white adobe structures of the pueblo sat in a somewhat random way, with lots of space in between them. This gave me a first impression of the town that was somehow welcoming, perhaps because it looked young and unfinished, and therefore still open to newcomers.

Then there was the Santa Barbara Mission, by far the biggest structure I'd ever seen. Even though located about a half-mile up from the beach, the mission stood out clearly as the largest building in town, looking from a distance like a combination of lighthouse and castle. As I later learned, an earthquake destroyed the original mission, and the current one, much larger and more detailed, was built about 1815–1820. The twin bell towers of the main chapel, with curved domed tops, are an impressive sight, especially to the eyes of someone like me who'd never seen anything like it. I wondered how the padres built something so big and elaborate in such a small, remote town.

I found the port captain's office—a small, two-room adobe close to the beach—walked in and saw two fellow Yankees sitting at a table, looking over a map. One was the captain, named Will Dana, and the other was Zack—the two men Yount told me about.

"Well, look at that, Will," said Zack, "seems like another Yankee just washed up on shore. Think he'll be as useless as the others?"

They both laughed at this comment, but before Dana responded I pulled out my letter of introduction and handed it to him.

"My friend George Yount seems to think I could be quite useful to you two gentlemen," I said.

This had the desired effect, as they stopped laughing, read the letter, and then offered their hands in introduction.

"We're the two men you are looking for," said Zack, "but better yet, you're just the man we've been looking for. Yount claims you're the best damn hunter he's ever seen."

Captain Dana apologized for the rude reception. He and Zack then explained why they were happy I'd come to Santa Barbara.

Apparently, the two had been trying to plan an otter hunting expedition, without much success. Dana was not much of a hunter, and as port captain couldn't be away for long periods. The dozen or so other Americans in town were in the trading or building business, and "couldn't shoot the side of a barn unless they were standing inside it."

The Spaniards and Mexicans were also not skilled hunters. Most came to this area to get into the cattle ranching business, or to work in some capacity for the Mexican government.

Will Dana was pleased because we would be hunting under his license, meaning he would get a percentage of our take. And Zack was happy to finally have an able hunting partner. So the timing of my arrival here was good. The otter were abundant, there was not much competition, and a big demand for "soft gold."

Zack offered to let me board at his house until I could find one of my own. That night, over some Mexican-made firewater, we got further acquainted and planned out our first hunt.

Zack was born in 1800 in a small town on the coast of Maine, about as far away from Santa Barbara as you could get in this country.

He was not as good a hunter as me, but had a lot of other useful skills and knowledge. He grew up near the ocean and was an expert sailor. His father was a blacksmith and a shipwright, and the two of them, after the death of Zack's mother, sailed a ship they had built themselves to St. Louis and settled there.

Zack, though, had the fever for hunting and trapping and roaming the wilderness and soon left St. Louis. After spending a few years in a hunting party led by the famous Jedediah Smith, he migrated to New Mexico and eventually came to the Los Angeles area of California. Mexican authorities there caught him hunting without a license and threw him in jail. However, Zack managed to escape and find an "unoccupied" canoe. He paddled his way up to Santa Barbara, knocking off a few otter on the way. Like me, once here he would never leave.

Will Dana had a more respectable entrance into town. He settled in Santa Barbara in 1825, was a Mexican citizen and married to a daughter of Don Carlos Carrillo, patriarch of one of the leading local families. Will first came here while the captain of a Boston-based trading vessel, and fell in love with both the town and his pretty wife, Josefa. He eventually received a 38,000 acre land grant, located near the Santa Maria River in San Luis Obispo County, now called the Casa de Dana Nipomo Rancho.

The next day Zack and I began preparing for our first otter hunt. He proposed we spend two weeks hunting in between Santa Barbara and Ventura.

I was surprised when Zack told me he planned to hire a couple of mission Indians to go along with us. I explained to him why I hated Indians and asked if we could do without them.

"Sorry, George," Zack said, "but you're in a much different place now. The missions pretty much wiped out the Indians around here. There is no reason to fear them, especially the ones who still live around the mission. They are completely trustworthy, and willing to do most anything to make some money.

"The two I'm hiring have worked for me before and believe me, you've got nothing to worry about. When you shoot an otter, they'll jump right into the water to retrieve it. They know how to skin, and cure the hides. They'll also cook and set up and strike camp.

"In short, these two Indians will help us shoot a lot more otter. And if it makes you feel better, be assured that the wages we pay them will be less than the extra money we'll make by having them work for us."

Even though I believed what Zack said, I was none too happy about it. Despite all the things I'd already seen and heard about the Indians' situation here in California, I wasn't yet ready to forget the past.

However, I did not argue with Zack about it. As he said, I was in a new place now. I had to accept his hiring of the two Indians. But it was still hard for me to look at any Indian and not think about Mark and Alex.

That first hunt with Zack lasted about two weeks. Although I really wasn't aware of it, during that hunt I began to lose my hatred of Indians, and even respect them. At the time I could not consciously admit this to myself. But now, looking back, I can see it was the beginning of a big change in the way I felt about Indians.

These two, like all Indians at the mission, had Spanish names—Miguel and Pedro. I was surprised when told they were brothers, as they didn't look or act alike. Miguel was tall and skinny, with a narrow face, long legs and arms, dark brown skin and black hair. He was very quiet and rarely spoke unless spoken to. He smiled a lot but rarely laughed.

Pedro was several inches shorter than his brother, with slightly lighter skin and hair. He was quite strong and muscular, and loved to laugh and make jokes, a bit like my new friend Zack.

The brothers, though, did share some things in common. Neither one ever showed any resentment about what happened to their people. They were also both devout Catholics, and very fond of Father Gonzalez, who was the head priest of the mission.

Miguel and Pedro were two of about a hundred Indians still living on land owned by Mission Santa Barbara (as I explained earlier, most of the mission land was taken by the Mexican government, but the padres still owned a few acres). Their parents, who'd both died of smallpox a few years earlier, were converts, and therefore Miguel and Pedro were born at the mission. Before being hired by Zack, their job was overseeing the mission's remaining farmland and small livestock operation.

When Zack first went to the mission to see about hiring someone, Father Gonzalez recommended these two. He hoped that working for hunters like us would give the brothers a chance to survive without the mission. Eventually, Gonzalez told Zack, the remaining land would be taken away, and he feared what would become of the Indians still living there.

During that hunt, I never spoke to Miguel and Pedro except when giving them a command. I made sure they knew I didn't like them and would've preferred to not have them around. However, as Zack promised, the two worked hard and were trustworthy. And even though I treated them with contempt, they never reciprocated such treatment in any way.

I also remember how impressed I was when first seeing the two brothers dive into the water to retrieve an otter. They could swim like dolphins and were absolutely fearless. They also handled a canoe as well as anyone.

Zack eventually became irritated by the way I treated the brothers. "You know, George, it wouldn't kill you to thank Miguel and Pedro once in a while for how hard they work."

"You might feel a little different about that if you'd experienced some of the things I have," I responded.

"Well, you might try remembering what Miguel and Pedro have gone through," said Zack. "Their tribe has been nearly wiped out. Their parents both died from smallpox—a white man's disease. The way I see it, they've got as much reason to hate you as you do them. But I don't see them making such a big deal about it."

I remember feeling angry when Zack said this. But I didn't try to argue the point, probably because I knew he was right.

When I first arrived in California, there were no sailing vessels here besides the American and British trading ships, which weren't available to charter for otter hunting.

So when Zack and I began hunting together, the only craft available to get us offshore was a canoe. Hunting in a canoe, once you became used to shooting from one, was a lot better than hunting from the beach—the canoes extended your range and made it easier to retrieve your prey once shot.

However, using these canoes to reach the islands, which we'd heard were thick with otter, was not an option. Even the islands closest to Santa Barbara—Anacapa, Santa Cruz, Santa Rosa and San Miguel—were twenty to thirty miles away.

"That's an ocean out there, not a big lake," Zack told me. "Oceans have strong currents, as well as unpredictable weather—storms and gales that move in with very little warning.

"Trying to make it out there in a canoe, well, I suppose if your life depended on it and the weather was perfect, you might make it. But there's still an excellent chance you'd end up as whale food. And besides, even if you did make it out there, you wouldn't be able to carry much back."

Again, though, my timing appeared to be good. A couple of months after I arrived here, word came to Santa Barbara that a wealthy ranchero down in the Los Angeles area had built a small schooner which he intended to lease out to various parties along the coast. We also heard he was looking for an experienced captain to lead an otter hunting expedition to Santa Cruz Island.

"Wish me luck, George," said Zack as he left for Los Angeles. "Hopefully, I'll be returning by ship."

While Zack was away, I decided to take a break from hunting and explore the area a bit. One day while walking near the mission, my eyes were suddenly drawn to the sight of a young señorita walking out of the chapel with a large group of people. She was absolutely gorgeous, and also elegantly dressed—a beautiful chemise with lace and embroidered sleeves, a muslin petticoat tied at the waist with a scarlet silk band, shoes of blue velvet, and a pearl necklace and earrings. Also, she had long, shiny black hair bouncing down her back.

I suddenly felt embarrassed by my mountain-man buckskins, dirty boots, and overgrown beard. Fortunately, she didn't notice me.

The sight of this particular señorita changed my outlook on things. To even meet such a woman, let alone enter a courtship, would require me to make some changes in life.

Her name was Sinforosa Sanchez, the daughter of a prominent ranchero, Don Ramon Sanchez. I found out from Will Dana, who knew everybody, that she was not yet engaged. Will advised me to be patient and not do anything until I was better known, held Mexican citizenship, and proved I was capable of providing for a wife and family.

"If you do these things, George, I'll arrange an introduction," Will promised.

"Oh, and there's one more requirement," he added. "You'll need to convert to Catholicism and be baptized. So you best get yourself some Sunday clothes and go introduce yourself to Father Gonzalez at the mission."

Well, I never believed I would ever become a Catholic, but in order to meet Señorita Sanchez, I was willing to give it a try. I started by doing something I'd never really done—pray. My first prayer was simple.

"God, please let Zack become captain of that schooner, and get back here soon."

Zack, or God, did not let me down. A few days after I saw Sinforosa for the first time, Will knocked on my door.

"George, I think you should come down to the beach."

When I got there, Zack was running a shoreboat up onto the beach with a big grin on his face. I didn't know what to think at first, but then I noticed a small schooner anchored about 150 yards offshore (back then, Santa Barbara didn't yet have a wharf or marina, so ships had to anchor offshore and use a "shoreboat" to deliver passengers and cargo onshore).

She was a modest little two-mast schooner, just twenty tons burthen and, according to Zack, not the best built ship he'd ever been on.

"She's not exactly the queen of the ocean, but I think she'll hold up well enough to get us out to those islands and shoot a few hundred otter or so!

"George, allow me to introduce you," Zack said as he pointed to the ship, "to the *Peor es Nada*."

I had to laugh, as the name in Spanish means "better than nothing." But it was a ship, and I could hardly wait to get on board, sail out to the islands, and start hunting otter.

However, as so often happens in life, just when you think everything is going your way, something unexpected occurs. There would be a delay in reaching our desired destination, and the hunting would have to wait.

Chapter Four

April 10, 1835

Before we started outfitting the *Peor es Nada* for otter hunting, Zack said he needed to discuss something with me.

"George, I'm going to be hiring Miguel and Pedro again. There is simply no way just the two of us can sail that ship, hunt and skin otter, and cook and clean. We need the help, and I know those two will do whatever we ask of them.

"So I need you to promise that you'll get along with them. On a ship as small as the *Peor es Nada*, it's very important that everyone is comfortable with each other and trusts one another. I won't have it any other way."

Well, I still wasn't ready to forgive and forget what happened in the past, but promised Zack I would get along with Miguel and Pedro. I had no choice. Without Zack as a hunting partner, I wouldn't be able to make a living here, and have a chance to meet a certain señorita. So I decided to do everything possible to hide my hatred of Indians until this trip was over.

Zack spent a couple of days teaching us the basics of sailing. I learned quickly, but was surprised to see Miguel and Pedro catching on even faster. They also performed every task with great care and enthusiasm. This didn't make it any easier for me to be nice to them.

Anyway, it was good that Zack got us well trained so

quickly, because a true test of our sailing skills came much sooner than expected.

The day before we planned to embark on a three-week otter hunt at Santa Cruz Island, a young Spaniard on horseback rode into town and approached me on the beach, where I was doing some last-minute waxing of the shoreboat. He asked where he could find Captain Sparks. I pointed to the port captain's office, where Will and Zack were copying a map for our trip. I saw him enter the office, and about five minutes later he came out, mounted his horse and rode away.

I had a feeling something was wrong, which was confirmed a few seconds later when Zack walked out of Dana's office and began kicking the sand. Looking up, he saw me and motioned me over.

"Sorry to tell you this, George, but that Spaniard who just left is the son of the owner of the *Peor es Nada,* and he came to inform us of a change in plans. It seems a couple of old Indians in a canoe just delayed our otter hunt!"

As we would later find out, the *Peor es Nada* was built with the help of Father Ramirez of the San Gabriel Mission in Los Angeles, who supplied Indians to do much of the work. So the owner owed Ramirez a favor, and that favor had just been called in.

Several days earlier at the San Pedro port in Los Angeles, a canoe was sighted far offshore. The two men in it struggled in their effort to reach the shore. After finally making it in they collapsed in the sand, obviously exhausted.

The port captain and a few Mission Indians went over to see who it was. They were surprised to find two rather old Indians wearing nothing but breechcloths made of yucca fiber, and shell necklaces. Even more surprising, the two had arrived in an Indian-made plank canoe. Such a canoe, which was much narrower and longer than the ones we used, hadn't been seen for many years. Inside the canoe were several large Indian water baskets, which were almost empty, and some dried abalone meat wrapped in seaweed.

It appeared they had traveled a long distance to get there. The port captain and the local Indians asked them where they were from, and why they had come. But the two old Indians could not answer, as they did not understand any Spanish or the language spoken by the Indians.

The port captain decided to take them to the San Gabriel Mission. Father Ramirez, through hand signs and with the aid of a map, finally solved the mystery.

The two old Indians had come in search of help for their tribe. There were just seventeen of them remaining, and only one child. They lived in a village on an island far across the ocean.

Ramirez showed the two Indians some maps, including one of the Channel Islands. After looking at it for a few moments, they pointed to San Nicolas Island.

Father Ramirez was amazed that these two old men traveled such a distance in a canoe, and touched by their obvious devotion to their people. He decided to do anything he could to help them.

And so our otter-hunting trip to Santa Cruz Island was delayed. We'd been ordered to first go to San Nicolas Island, remove the remaining Indians there and take them to the San Gabriel Mission.

"It makes me wonder," said Zack. "Ever since landing

in Santa Barbara, I've dreamt of finding a ship that could get us out to the islands. I know there's a ton of soft gold out there, just waiting for us. Then I finally find one, and something like this happens."

"Well, the otter aren't going anywhere," I said, "and the trip to San Nicolas shouldn't take us more than a few days."

"Yeah, I know you're probably right," said Zack, "but for some reason I'm worried it'll delay us longer than that."

I then suggested we consider making a slight detour on our way out to San Nicolas.

"You know, Zack, we'll be going right by Santa Cruz on the way to San Nicolas. Why not take a day or two to scout the island, and see where the otter lay? That will save us time later on, and I don't think the owner of the *Peor es Nada* would mind too much if we knock off a few otter while we're there."

Zack thought about this for a few seconds then shook his head.

"No, George," he said. "It's tempting, but I just want to get the trip to San Nicolas over and done with as quickly as possible."

We left for San Nicolas early in the morning of April 10, 1835. It was clear and calm when we set out, but around the time we passed by Santa Cruz Island several hours later, the wind picked up a bit and clouds began to roll in from the northwest. I asked Zack if it was anything to worry about.

"Too soon to tell," he said, "and the truth is I haven't spent enough time in these parts to really know the weather."

"What happens," I asked him, "if we get to San Nicolas

and a storm or gale hits?"

"If conditions get too rough, we won't be able to use the shoreboat, which means we won't be able to get the Indians off the island. In that case, we've got two choices. We can drop anchor and wait for calmer weather. Or we can leave and go wait it out elsewhere."

"Why wouldn't we just stay at San Nicolas?" I asked.

"Several reasons. We don't know if San Nicolas has a good harbor—somewhere safe to wait out a storm. If it does, we won't know where it is, or if it's on the leeward side of the island."

Zack then pointed at the ship's anchor. "That anchor is another reason. It's a little too small for my liking. If we're in a heavy gale or storm with no protection, it may start to drag. If that happens, we'll have to set sail."

"Back to the Santa Barbara Channel?" I asked.

"No," Zack said. "Probably just back to Santa Cruz. That island has several good harbors, and we know where they are. But it also depends on which direction the wind is blowing. If it's from the north or the west, it may be safer and quicker to head to San Pedro—it's the closest point on the mainland from San Nicolas."

On the way out, Zack asked Miguel and Pedro how they felt about going out to San Nicolas to remove the last of the island-dwelling Indians. They both shrugged and said nothing for a few moments. Finally, Pedro responded.

"It will be sad to see them leave the island. I know they can no longer survive there, but I wonder if living at the mission will be any better for them."

Then Miguel spoke. "California is now a very difficult place for Indians to survive, especially if they can't speak

Spanish. It will be hard for them to find work, and stay together as a people."

A few hours after passing by Santa Cruz, the island of San Nicolas came into sight. When it first appeared on the horizon, some questions came to mind I've never been able to answer. How did this island, way out in the middle of the ocean, and so far away from another body of land, ever come into existence? How and when was it formed? How long ago did the Indians discover it, and why would they ever want to live on such a remote island?

Even though much smaller than Santa Cruz, San Nicolas is still a pretty big chunk of land—about eight-miles long and three-miles across at its widest point. It is somewhat oval-shaped, the two ends pointing northwest and southeast, with a slight northward curve on the upper end.

Running down the middle of the island is a ridge about three hundred feet high, and perhaps six miles in length, with numerous ravines and canyons sloping down each side. The lower end of the island is mostly flat and sandy, with a half-mile long point sticking out of the west end.

I am not sure why, but San Nicolas does not have any big trees or areas that could be called a forest. Perhaps it's due to the constant ocean wind or the soil, which is sandy and thin. However, much of the island is covered with moss and many kinds of small plants and bushes, so it displays a mostly green color. The base of the island is largely made up of white-sand beaches, though some areas instead have craggy, rocky cliffs marked by cave mouth openings of various sizes.

The sizeable main ridge apparently catches a lot of rainwater, as the island has many springs around the lower areas.

I would suppose there is enough fresh water to maintain a large population. But according to what the two old men in the canoe told Father Ramirez, there were now just fifteen Indians remaining there.

We hoped that the remaining "Nicoleños"—the name by which Miguel and Pedro called them—would be ready to leave quickly and that the wind would lessen before we tried to get them off the island. Unfortunately, neither of these things happened.

About mid-afternoon, as we got within a mile or so of San Nicolas, the weather suddenly shifted. What had been a moderate to heavy breeze all day grew stronger and changed directions, blowing from the west.

I began to wonder if the wind was getting too strong to safely use the shoreboat. Like Zack, I was anxious to get this trip over and done with, but I was not going to get into the shoreboat if it got too windy. "There's no way," I thought to myself, "I'm going to risk my life to save a bunch of worthless Indians."

As we got within a few hundred yards of the island, we spotted someone walking down a path to a broad, white-sand beach.

"Okay!" Zack shouted. "It looks like the Nicoleños know we're here. Let's drop anchor, untie the shoreboat and get this done as quickly as possible."

The plan was for Zack to stay on board the *Peor es Nada*, and for me, Miguel and Pedro to row the shoreboat in, load the Indians, and row back to the ship. I looked at Miguel and Pedro, and saw a bit of fear in their faces. The wind was growing stronger by the minute, and the waves rolling into shore were now whitecapped. I think they were wondering the same thing I was—even if we got the shoreboat safely to shore, would we be able to get back to the ship through those oncoming waves?

I think Zack sensed our anxiety, and did his best to assure us we would be okay. "C'mon, don't worry, we can do this! Just make sure that on the way back to the ship you keep the shoreboat headed straight into the waves. And once you get over the crest of one wave, row like hell until you hit the next one."

As we lowered the shoreboat down into the water, a gust of wind hit us, rocking the ship and causing Miguel to lose his balance and almost fall overboard. I looked at Zack and asked him, "are you sure about this?" His response didn't exactly reassure me.

"George, stop asking questions and get moving! The way the wind is picking up we may not have much time left to get this done."

The shoreboat was big enough to safely take four Nicoleños at a time, so it would require four trips to get them all to the ship. It would be my job to push the shoreboat as far as possible into the surf, and then up to Miguel and Pedro to row it back to the ship. Once they left the shore, I would get the next four Nicoleños ready.

As we neared the shore, we were disappointed to see just one Indian waiting for us. He was a rather old man who looked somewhat frightened. It made me think that the Nicoleños had reason to fear strangers arriving at their island, and couldn't tell whether or not we were there to help them.

When we landed on the beach, the old man slowly approached us and spoke a few words. Pedro and Miguel could not understand his language. Then they tried speaking to him, but with the same result.

Finally, Miguel kneeled down and with his finger drew the shape of a canoe in the sand, pointed at the old man and put up two fingers. He then pointed out to the *Peor es Nada* and the old man seemed to finally understand that his two fellow Nicoleños had succeeded in finding help, and that we meant to take the rest of them off the island.

Through more signs we tried to make him understand that due to the strong wind, we were in a hurry to go. He seemed to understand this, and turned and ran away up a path leading from the beach towards the interior of the island. We watched him go over a ridge and then could not see him after that. We walked up and down the beach a bit and looked up at various parts of the island, but could not see the location of the Nicoleños' village.

"I hope he understands we're in a hurry," said Miguel, "and I also hope their village is not too far away."

After waiting for about twenty minutes, during which time the wind picked up considerably, the three of us had become even more nervous. We knew if conditions worsened any further, getting back to the ship might be an impossible and perhaps even deadly undertaking. I remember thinking I was about to get stuck on an island with a bunch of Indians, which was not exactly a dream come true for me.

I tried to put such thoughts out of my mind and trust the decision our captain had made. But then we looked out to the ship and saw Zack making motions with his arms. We weren't sure, but it looked like he was signaling us to get in the shoreboat and return to the ship.

Just at that time, though, the Nicoleños finally arrived at the beach. We were surprised to see just two men among them—a young adult and the old man who met us on the beach. Of the women, only two or three were old.

They all carried large baskets filled with various items, such as stone cooking vessels, coils of sinew rope, shell necklaces and small figurines. I couldn't help but think what a strange time it must be for these people. They were leaving the only home they'd ever known, taking with them only what they could carry, without knowing anything about their destination. What thoughts were going through their minds I could only imagine.

Miguel, Pedro and I looked at each other, uncertain of what to do. The Nicoleños had finally arrived, but we were no longer sure if we could get them all safely to the ship.

"Let's get the first group loaded, and see how it goes," suggested Miguel. "We've come all the way out here, and the Nicoleños are ready to go."

Pedro nodded his head in agreement, and then looked at me. After a brief moment of hesitation, I shrugged my shoulders and said, "what the hell, let's give it a try."

When I look back on that day now, I wonder why we were all in such a damn hurry. When that gale started to hit, why didn't Zack decide to turn the ship around, sail to a safe spot, and wait until calm weather returned? And why did the two brothers and I decide to go ahead and start transporting the Nicoleños out to the *Peor es Nada*? We could've just gone back to the ship and told Zack we weren't willing to risk our lives to do something that was not urgent.

After all, the Nicoleños weren't going anywhere. And neither were the otter at Santa Cruz Island. A delay of a day or two wouldn't have mattered at all.

I suppose it's just a sad fact of human nature. Especially in our younger days, we tend to be in a hurry when we really don't need to be. And when that happens, we sometimes make bad decisions—decisions that can change lives and even alter the course of history.

And so we loaded the first group of Nicoleños into the shoreboat. As Pedro and Miguel started to row back to the *Peor es Nada*, I noticed that only thirteen Nicoleños had arrived on the beach—there should've been fifteen. Where were the other two?

Also, we were told that one of the remaining Nicoleños was a child, but there were no children among the group on the beach.

One other thing also caught my eye—a pack of seven or eight dogs, which I saw running across a long plateau just below the main ridge of the island. They looked like coyotes, except they were of a black and white color. I wondered whether they were wild or tame, and how they got there.

As I watched Miguel and Pedro battle through the waves, I noticed the Nicoleños looking very worried about something. They were talking rapidly to each other and pointing at different parts of the island. Even though I couldn't understand their language, I knew what they were concerned about—not everyone in their tribe had made it to the beach.

By then, the wind had become so strong it whipped up the sand, and the ocean swell so heavy that the ship almost disappeared from sight in between waves. Miguel and Pedro struggled mightily to row the shoreboat out to the *Peor es Nada*, unload the Nicoleños, and row back in to shore.

As they returned for the second group, the remaining Nicoleños were growing more concerned about the missing ones. Then one of the young Nicoleño women said something to the others, and took off running up the path that led away from the beach.

Within about twenty minutes, Miguel and Pedro completed three trips to the ship and were on their way back in. The only ones left were the old man and myself, but then the woman who'd left earlier returned. She said something to the old man while shaking her head and trying to catch her breath.

By the time Miguel and Pedro arrived back on the beach, the wind was so strong we had to shout to hear each other. Pedro began yelling at me to hurry up and get the last Nicoleños loaded into the shoreboat.

"Zack said the anchor is starting to drag and the wind is blowing the ship away from the island. We can't wait any longer!"

I then turned to the old man and the young woman, who looked unsure of what to do. They were hesitant to leave the island, but at the same time knew that we were about to leave, and most of their people were on board the ship.

Pedro made the decision for them. He took their baskets and loaded them into the shoreboat. He then made motions to the man and woman to climb in, which they reluctantly did. Miguel and Pedro quickly followed them and grabbed the oars while I pushed the shoreboat into the surf and jumped in. Then the brothers began pulling on those oars with all their might.

Upon approaching the ship, I could see Zack was in a panic. As he'd suspected, the anchor was not heavy enough to keep the *Peor es Nada* in place, and she was rocking and bobbing so severely I didn't think we'd be able to get back on board.

APRIL 10, 1835

The shoreboat was nearly impossible to control and almost capsized several times. Finally, though, we got close enough to the ship to unload, and Zack threw the rope ladder down to us. It was only due to Pedro's remarkable strength that the rest of us were able to climb on board. He held onto the rope ladder with one hand while boosting us off the boat, one by one, with the other hand. He then tied the shoreboat rope around his waist and pulled himself up.

The Nicoleños, except of course the two missing ones, were now on board, and huddled together below deck. Zack began shouting commands, and we all scrambled around the swaying ship to get the shoreboat secured, the anchor up, and the sails unfurled.

As the *Peor es Nada* began to head away from the island, Miguel went down below deck to calm our passengers, and attempt through hand signals to assure them we would come back later to pick up the two missing ones.

While he was doing this, Zack was at the helm and Pedro and I were just behind him, amidships on the starboard side. We both kneeled down to make sure the shoreboat was securely tied down. When I stood up, I broke one of the cardinal rules of sailing in rough seas—I did not grab hold of anything to secure my footing.

Just as I realized this, the port side of the *Peor es Nada* took on a large swell, causing the ship to lurch over to the starboard side. I suddenly lost my balance and stumbled over the shoreboat. Then, as I tried to stand up and turn around to grab the rail, I slipped and fell back head-first over the side of the ship.

It's funny, at times like this, how thoughts can so quickly run through your head. From the moment I first realized I was falling off the ship to the moment I actually hit the water was just a split second. And yet, in that brief moment all of the following thoughts came to me:

First—I was wearing boots and thick clothing, which would make it nearly impossible for me to swim in such conditions.

Next—Pedro was probably the only one who saw me fall overboard. After the way I'd treated him, he'd probably be happy to see me drown.

Strangely enough, I realized, for the first time that day, that it was my birthday. I was going to drown on my birthday!

And then the worst thought of all—I was going to drown because of a bunch of damned Indians on some distant, god-forsaken island.

I hit the turbulent sea head first in a trough between two huge swells. The immense power of the water spun me around and down so I wasn't even sure which way was up. I instinctively tried to take a breath, but inhaled only water. I kicked my legs and swung my arms in a desperate effort to get my head above water.

It seemed like an eternity, but was probably just a few seconds later when I felt cold air on my face. In the brief moment I had my head above water I tried in vain to suck in some air and locate the ship. And then I went under again.

There's nothing quite like the feeling of thinking you're about to die and there's nothing you can do about it. At that point, images of my family and other scenes from my past spun through my mind.

But then I heard a splash in the water, very close to me. At first I thought it must be some creature of the sea, but a few seconds later I felt a pair of hands grab me under the arms from behind and pull me upward.

Suddenly I was moving through the water, and realized that whoever had grabbed me was tied to the end of a rope. Then I felt myself rising out of the sea, still being held under the arms. I heard Zack's voice yelling "pull, pull, pull!" and I swung around, was let go from behind, and landed on the deck of the *Peor es Nada*.

For the next few moments I was face down on my knees, desperately trying to clear my lungs and hanging on with all my might to the stern rail. And that's when I looked up and saw the woman on the plateau, and the pack of dogs running up a trail in her direction. Then I turned around and saw Pedro smiling at me in his wet clothes.

It all happened so quickly. In just about a minute's time, I fell overboard, thought I was about to die and then was rescued, saw the woman who was left behind, and realized an Indian just saved my life.

I felt somehow different as I stood up to resume my duties aboard the *Peor es Nada*. Perhaps I already sensed I was a changed man, and that the journey begun on April 10, 1835, was far from over.

Chapter Five

Alone and Forgotten

Our voyage to San Pedro was like a bad dream that wouldn't end. Nightfall came soon after leaving San Nicolas, and the gale continued to grow stronger. The windswept ocean was a dark, endless succession of huge swells and deep troughs. As ships are wont to do in such conditions, the *Peor es Nada* creaked and groaned, reminding me of Zack's comment that "she's not exactly the queen of the ocean." I was gripped by a continuous state of fear and dread, certain that the ship was going to break apart and sink.

The Nicoleños, surprisingly, showed no fear at all. I went below deck several times that night to dry off a bit, and when I looked at them they appeared very calm, as if used to such terrifying circumstances.

The four of us worked ceaselessly to keep the *Peor es Nada* before the wind and avoid capsizing. The spray of the waves and the incessant wind made it difficult to stay dry and keep our lanterns lit. I was chilled to the bone, exhausted, and uncertain if I would see the light of day again.

Throughout that long night, I was also troubled by what happened earlier. I couldn't quite believe that an Indian saved my life—and risked his own to do so. Zack later explained to me how quickly Pedro moved to get a coil of rope, throw one end to Zack and then jump overboard to rescue me. I suddenly felt guilty about how I'd been treating Pedro, and also about certain things I'd done in the past.

I also thought often of the woman left behind. The sight of her up on that plateau kept coming to mind. What caused her to arrive too late to get on the ship? Did it have something to do with the child? Or with the pack of dogs?

Finally, I saw the first light of dawn appear over the mountains east of Los Angeles. Just after that, the wind died down and the ocean became much calmer. We were going to make it after all.

I looked at Miguel and Pedro. They were smiling, no doubt feeling the same sense of relief I was.

"So, Señor George, how was your night?" asked Pedro, and I couldn't help but smile, too.

"Well," I said, "it was so damn miserable that at times I was wishing you'd let me drown."

I wanted to thank Pedro for what he'd done, and apologize for how I'd been treating him and Miguel, but I struggled to get the words out.

"Pedro, I know I haven't been very nice to you and Miguel, and I …"

"It's okay, Señor George. You don't have to thank me. I know you would do the same thing for me," he said, still smiling.

"Until yesterday, probably not," I said. "But from now on, if you ever do something really stupid like fall overboard during a heavy gale, I'll give serious consideration to jumping in after you."

We both laughed, and for a moment our eyes met. For the first time in my life, I was looking at an Indian and seeing nothing more or nothing less than another human being.

Just before arriving in San Pedro, I told the others about seeing the woman, and the pack of dogs, as we sailed away from San Nicolas. Zack then told us there was something he wanted to say.

"Don't feel bad if you were frightened last night. You should always be afraid of the sea. It's a very dangerous place to be. You must respect it, and never take unnecessary risks—like I did yesterday.

"I kept on going to San Nicolas when I should've turned back. As a result I put our lives in danger. And because we didn't get everyone off that island, we'll have to go back, which means I put our lives in danger for nothing."

I told Zack to not be too hard on himself, and pointed out that if the woman and child had arrived with the rest of the Nicoleños we would've gotten everyone off the island.

"I suppose you're right, George. Anyway, we can't change what's already happened. All we can do now is try to figure out what to do next."

"Won't we go right back to San Nicolas?" asked Pedro.

No one spoke for a few moments. Having just experienced such a terrifying and exhausting night of sailing, the thought of heading back out to San Nicolas was not too appealing.

Finally, it was the normally quiet Miguel who spoke.

"Every day the woman and child spend out there will be a day of hardship and loneliness. I think we should return right away."

"So do I," said Zack, "but remember, this is not our ship. All we can do is tell the owner and Father Ramirez what happened, and hope they agree."

Like the port of Santa Barbara, San Pedro at that time

did not have a wharf or marina, so we anchored offshore and started to transport the Nicoleños with the shoreboat.

Some of them were too weary and weak to climb down the ladder from the ship to the boat. However, the one young male Nicoleño carried the ailing ones on his back and got everyone safely off board.

He was extremely strong and muscular, probably about thirty-years-old, and had a long scar on one side of his face, running all the way from his hairline to below his jaw. I wondered what could've caused such a wound.

I also wondered why, among the remaining sixteen adult Nicoleños, there was only one young man, and four men total, and why most of the women were of a fairly young age. Was one of them the mother of the child, or was it the woman who was left behind? We could not get answers to such questions, as the Nicoleños apparently spoke a language no one else could understand.

We took them to the San Pedro port captain's office and sent word to Father Ramirez and the owner of the *Peor es Nada* that we'd arrived. It was interesting to see the reaction of these island people to the many things they were seeing for the first time. When someone on horseback passed by, they stopped and stared at the horse in wonder. Some of them laughed and one of the women indicated to us that she wanted to try riding it.

At the port captain's office, a small stucco building with an adobe tile roof, they spent a lot of time examining the solid walls and wooden doors, and looked like they were trying to figure out how such a structure was built.

The Nicoleños were also curious about this new land they had just arrived in. They gazed at the mountains to the east and up and down the coastline. Having spent their entire lives on San Nicolas Island, they probably did not know they had come to a place that was not an island, but rather a continent that went on for thousands of miles.

Everyone who saw the Nicoleños stopped and stared at them. They were dressed in capes of otter skins, with trousers and skirts of woven yucca fiber, and ornamented with feathers and shell beads. The Indians around here had stopped wearing such clothing and ornaments years before, having replaced them with the plain gray or brown trousers, shirts and dresses made at the missions.

While waiting, I saw something I'd never seen before—an Indian canoe, sitting behind the port captain's office. It was the canoe in which the two old Nicoleños traveled from San Nicolas Island to San Pedro.

It was about twelve-feet long, made of planks about eight-inches wide and two-inches thick, and with a narrower, deeper design than the canoes we used for otter hunting. The planks had been beveled and grooved to fit perfectly together. The seams were sealed with heated bitumen. The ends of the planks had small holes through which a type of twine was inserted to sew them together, and the hull was covered with pitch to keep it from absorbing water.

There was only one cross member, a beam which braced the hull in the middle of the craft. The gunwales were open in a V shape at the bow and stern. I suppose this was done so a rope or fishing line could be let through. Washboards were sewn in at both ends, which would deflect water in heavy surf or rough seas.

It was extremely light for its size, and therefore would require perfect coordination among the rowers, and also some kind of ballast to keep it stable.

The port captain saw me admiring this canoe, and came

over to tell me that the day before a couple of local hunters tried to use it.

"They took about five strokes before capsizing," he told me. "They kept trying and the canoe kept dumping them into the water. When they finally gave up and came in, I couldn't help but ask them how a couple of old Indians went seventy miles in that canoe, and they couldn't go ten feet!"

"It's hard to believe," I said. "They must have had calm weather, but even so—seventy miles over open ocean in a *canoe*."

"Well, as you can see," he replied, "it's not at all like the ordinary canoes we use. Imagine the time and skill and experience it took to build such a craft, and to learn how to use it.

"Take a good look at it," he said, walking away, "it's probably the last of its kind."

When I first saw Father Ramirez and the owner of the *Peor es Nada*, I had a feeling they would agree to let us return directly to San Nicolas. Both of them seemed very concerned about the Nicoleños, and Father Ramirez told us he would do whatever possible to help them adapt to their new surroundings.

He brought with him the two old men, and their reunion with the other Nicoleños was a happy scene, although it didn't last long. As soon as the two old men found out that two members of their tribe were still on San Nicolas they became quite upset. They came over to us and through signs and gestures appeared to be asking if we would go back to San Nicolas. We tried to indicate that we planned to do so, but didn't yet know when we would go.

I couldn't help but feel sorry for the Nicoleños. They no longer had a home or a place to call their own, and were in a completely different world where no one could understand their language. And two members of their tribe, including the only child, were now separated from the rest.

I recalled what Miguel said when Zack asked him how he felt about removing the last of the Channel Island Indians. "California has become a very difficult place for Indians to survive ... and it will be hard for them to stay together as a people." I wondered, had the Nicoleños known what Miguel did about California, if they would've decided to just stay put on San Nicolas.

I saw Zack discussing something with the owner of the *Peor es Nada*. I assumed he was asking if we could return to San Nicolas before going otter hunting. After listening to the owner for a few minutes, Zack nodded his head but looked somehow disappointed.

As it turned out, my feeling about immediately returning to San Nicolas was wrong. Zack came over and explained why.

The owner had agreed to let us return to San Nicolas, but before doing so he wanted us to make a couple of other trips. Therefore, the next morning, we would be setting sail—destination San Francisco.

Here is what caused the change in plans:

The wife of the owner of the *Peor es Nada* had a sister who was married to a wealthy ranchero in the San Francisco Area. Their rancho had recently been robbed by a group of Indian bandits.

The Indians came in the middle of the night. They broke into the main hacienda where the ranchero and his family slept, and held them at gunpoint while stealing nearly everything of value—gold and silver coins, jewelry, even clothing. The bandits then released all of the livestock and herded them off the rancho. Most of the animals were never recovered.

News of this robbery slowly spread through California, and reached the owner of the *Peor es Nada* the day we left for San Nicolas. He and his wife wanted to help their relatives, who suddenly had lost most of their wealth. And so we'd been ordered to deliver a leather pouch full of gold and silver coins to them at their rancho near San Francisco.

Then we were to go to Santa Cruz Island, and hunt there until we had at least one hundred skins. After delivering those to San Pedro, we could then head back to San Nicolas.

We were all disappointed by this decision. I looked at Miguel and Pedro, and saw a bit of anger in their eyes. I knew what they were thinking—if the two people left behind on San Nicolas weren't Indians, a different decision would've been made.

"I suppose I can't blame him," said Zack. "After all, he spent a lot of money to build the *Peor es Nada,* and so far all she's being used for is rescuing people and delivering money. Also, remember that it was me, not him, who decided to keep on going to San Nicolas Island when we should've turned back. So I'm really the one to blame for this happening."

"Anyway, what's done is done," I said. "We can't change the situation. All we can do is hope the woman and child can survive until we return."

"The trip to San Francisco and the otter hunting should take about a month," said Zack. "That's assuming all goes according to plan. And as we know from what happened yesterday, that doesn't always happen."

We had good weather on our trip to San Francisco, with the advantage of a steady following wind. After the horrific voyage from San Nicolas, it was a relief to sail under such ideal conditions. It also gave us time to discuss the question of whether the woman and child could survive until we returned.

First, we acknowledged it would be impossible to know their chances of survival without knowing the age of the child. Was it an infant who would be a burden? Or an older child who could be of help?

Another question we couldn't answer—why was the woman alone when I saw her on that plateau? Whatever the age of the child, why wasn't it with her?

The one thing we did know is that the woman had lived on San Nicolas her whole life. She would know how to get food and water. Wouldn't that be all she really needed to survive until we returned?

Perhaps not—one more unknown was the pack of dogs I saw. If they were wild, would the woman and child be in danger of getting attacked by them?

I asked Miguel and Pedro about their attempts to talk to the Nicoleños.

"We couldn't understand a single word," said Miguel. "The Nicoleños speak a language we have never heard before."

"We thought the Indians out on the islands were all Chumash," said Pedro. "But it is not so. I think the Nicoleños originally came from a different place.

"In the past, I'm sure they traded and married with the

Chumash, so there would've been those who could speak both languages. But then the missionaries came, which changed everything for the Indians. Now our tribes are almost gone. So there are probably no Chumash left who can speak the Nicoleño tongue, and the remaining Nicoleños don't understand any language but their own."

As we neared San Francisco, Zack looked a little bit nervous, and I asked him why.

"Not nervous at all, George. I'm very relaxed right now, as I always am when sailing into a very dangerous bay for the first time, with a crew that's spent a total of five days at sea."

"What's so dangerous about San Francisco Bay?"

"Well, I hear it's one of the greatest natural harbors ever discovered—a huge bay, protected by two large peninsulas. However, the entrance to the bay is said to be full of reefs, sand bars, barely submerged boulders, and strong tidal flows. It's also often fogged in, there's no lighthouse, and no map showing where the hazards lay.

"I'm also a bit worried about the rudder—or more specifically, the rudder post, which connects the rudder to the tiller. I'll show you."

Zack then had me take the tiller, and told me to turn it back and forth. As I did so, I felt a vibration in my hands.

"Feel that vibration?" Zack asked me. "It indicates a problem in the attachment of the rudder to the rudder post—perhaps a crack in the wood, or a loose tendon. It's still working okay, but if it breaks before we can dock the ship and fix the problem, we'll be in big trouble.

"It should hold up until we get to San Francisco, and repairing it won't take more than a few days, if we're lucky."

I remember thinking that the four of us on the *Peor es Nada* weren't the ones who really needed the luck, but rather those two out on that island. Their luck had not been so good so far.

The entrance into San Francisco Bay is through a wide channel, now called the Golden Gate, in between two peninsulas, San Mateo on the south (San Francisco sits on its northern tip) and Marin to the north. As we approached the Golden Gate, conditions looked good—it was mid-afternoon, the sky was clear and the wind calm.

However, I can tell you now, as I look back on that day, that somehow I knew something bad was about to happen, although I can't really say why. Maybe the feeling came from all the things already gone wrong—the last-minute delay of our otter-hunting plans, the gale that hit us at San Nicolas, the absence of the woman and child while loading the Nicoleños, the decision to send us to San Francisco and Santa Cruz before returning to San Nicolas, and the problem with the ship's rudder.

I tried to convince myself that everything was alright, and this feeling resulted from my lack of time on board a ship—just part of the process of becoming a seasoned sailor.

Then, while approaching the eastern corner of the San Mateo peninsula, we saw the fog. At first, we couldn't see the extent of it, but upon entering the Golden Gate we saw fog over the entire bay and most of the peninsula. It blocked our view of San Francisco, and was spreading in our direction.

This huge fog bank was quite a sight and as I now know, not an unusual one for the San Francisco Bay. It looked like a huge cloud had dropped down out of the sky and spread itself across the bay and peninsula. From where we were, there was only about a mile of visibility before everything disappeared into a vast whiteness.

Zack shook his head in disgust. "Finding your way though fog like that is impossible," he said. "We'll have to just stay put for a while and wait until it clears. I'll get us a little closer to shore and then we'll drop anchor."

Zack then pushed the tiller to steer the *Peor es Nada* towards the shore, and at that moment we heard a loud thump come from below the ship. I looked at Zack and saw him struggling to move the tiller. He yelled at me to come over and help him, which I did, but even with both of us pushing it wouldn't move.

Suddenly the ship veered toward the shore. We quickly began to drop our sails and prepare to heave anchor. While doing this, as we were about two hundred yards offshore, the *Peor es Nada* started to vibrate and shake, and make a sound like something was banging into the hull. Then the bow rose up a few feet, and she came to a complete stop. We heard the sound of water rushing into the hold, and the ship began to slowly tip over on her starboard side.

The *Peor es Nada* had run into a rock reef, ripping a large gash in the hull, and was quickly taking on water. Our first concern was our cargo. Zack and I ran down into the hold and grabbed the money pouch, our rifles, bullets and powder. While doing so Zack yelled at Pedro and Miguel to untie the shoreboat. But before they could do so, the *Peor es Nada* capsized, dumping us all into the water.

As we started to swim, I looked towards the shore and saw nothing but a high, steep cliff. Fortunately, though, the tide was out, so there was an area of open beach at the foot of the cliff. The water was also mercifully calm that day.

It was slow going as we swam through the frigid water. Even though all of us were good swimmers, we were fully clothed, wearing boots, and all holding on to some item from the ship.

I experienced a brief moment of panic, probably caused by my near-drowning just a few days prior. But I soon relaxed, realizing that conditions were dramatically different, and that as long as I kept my head above water I would be okay.

As we all finally made it ashore, I felt a jumble of emotions. We had lost our ship, but at least we were alive. Then I thought about the two Nicoleños. Was their chance of being rescued sinking along with the *Peor es Nada*?

As we staggered to our feet, I saw that Pedro had the foresight to have grabbed a large coil of rope from the ship. He then volunteered to climb up the sixty feet or so of mostly sheer cliff. This was a nerve-wracking thing to watch, as he slipped and nearly fell several times. We also knew the tide would reverse, and if we couldn't get to higher ground we'd be swept right back into the ocean.

But Pedro made it to the top, secured the rope and began pulling the rest of us up. Once this was done, we looked back down at the *Peor es Nada*. It was still afloat, but slowly sinking and almost upside down in the water as it drifted away. We could clearly see the puncture made in the hull by the reef.

The four of us just stood there for a while, in our drenched clothing, and no one spoke. I think we needed a few minutes to think about what just happened, and what to do next.

Zack sat down on a rock and put his head in his hands.

I knew he was blaming himself for losing the ship, even though it was due to a faulty rudder. I wanted to say something to make him feel better, but could think of nothing.

As I said, sometimes when life seems to be going your way, something unexpected occurs. Just a few days earlier, we were about to set out for three weeks of otter hunting. But now, we found ourselves on a cliff above the Golden Gate, without a ship and worried about the fate of two people on a distant island.

"Farewell, young lady," Zack said sadly as he looked down at the *Peor es Nada*. Then he stood up and we all started walking towards San Francisco.

We came on shore a few miles away from our intended destination. The terrain was mostly flat and not too thickly forested, but we suddenly found ourselves enveloped by fog and had to stop until it lifted. Soon darkness came, and we had to spend the night in a makeshift camp, with no food or blankets. At least, though, we were able to start a fire, dry out a bit, and discuss what to do next.

"Let's hope there's a ship in port that's about to head down south," said Zack, "or one available to charter. Otherwise, we'll have to buy some horses."

"I'm in favor of returning by horseback," said Pedro. "At least that way I won't have to swim through the ocean or climb up any cliffs to get home."

"Pedro, I know you're joking, but I agree," I said. "I've had enough of the sea for awhile. But a ship will get us home faster than a horse. It's now been almost a week since we left San Nicolas, and it'll take awhile to get back to Santa Barbara. I wonder how long the woman and child can survive out on that island."

"An even better question," said Zack, "is can we find another ship to get us back out there?"

The next morning the fog cleared enough for us to find our way to San Francisco, which back then was not much bigger than Santa Barbara. It wouldn't become such a big city until the discovery of gold in 1848.

After arriving we went to see the port captain, an American named William Richardson, who I'd briefly met when here before. He was surprised to see me back in San Francisco, and even more surprised to hear how I'd arrived. He told us there were no ships available to charter, and the next trading vessel wasn't due to arrive in San Francisco for another three weeks.

So he gave us directions to the mission, where we could buy horses and some provisions for our trip home. Before leaving, we told Richardson about the two Indians left behind on San Nicolas, and asked him to tell the captain of any ship heading down south to contact us if that ship was available to charter.

The padres at Mission Dolores in San Francisco were quite inhospitable. We explained to them our situation, but they seemed not to care. They did not offer us any food or provisions, and demanded a large sum of money to sell us four horses not in the best of condition.

The Indians living around this mission looked much worse off than the ones at Mission Santa Barbara. I asked Miguel and Pedro about this.

"Some of the missions," said Miguel, "are run by priests who have no respect for Indians. Others are run by those like Father Gonzalez in Santa Barbara. He works hard and always thinks of others first."

"The missions failed to help Indians," added Pedro, "because most of the padres failed to see us as real human beings. It is as simple as that."

Before heading back to Santa Barbara we went to deliver the money to the family of the owner of the *Peor es Nada*. This turned out to be a somewhat unpleasant experience.

As we approached the main gate of the rancho, two vaqueros on horseback rode up, aiming their rifles at us. It was not exactly the welcome we expected. Zack quickly explained to them why we were there, but at first they did not believe him. They wanted to see the money, and even after doing so continued to keep their rifles up as they escorted us to the main hacienda.

The owners came out and greeted us with a suspicious look. Not until we handed over the money did the vaqueros drop their rifles. The owners invited Zack and me to supper with them, but made it clear that Miguel and Pedro were not included in the invitation. I was relieved but not surprised when Zack politely declined—after having rifles aimed at us and Miguel and Pedro treated in such a way, we were ready to be moving on.

"I feel sorry for them," said Pedro as we left the rancho. I was surprised by this comment and asked him why he felt that way.

"As you can see, they are living in fear and afraid of everyone. They do not understand why the Indians robbed them. And why it may happen again."

Pedro then explained that many Indians in California were starving—they had no money, no land, and could not find work.

"Before the Spaniards came," he said, "Indians never stole anything. There was no reason to ever do such a thing, because our land and the ocean provided everything we needed to live. But now, stealing from the ranchos is for many the only way to survive."

To get back to Santa Barbara we traveled along the *El Camino Real*, basically a trail or path connecting the missions, which were on average about twenty-five to thirty miles apart. We therefore saw about a dozen missions in between San Francisco and Santa Barbara.

At some of them we received generous hospitality, and the padres happily fed and boarded us. Three of them, after hearing the story of the woman and child on San Nicolas Island, and the sinking of the *Peor es Nada*, insisted on giving us fresh horses to help us get back sooner. The missions where we received such treatment were in good condition, and the Indians there seemed fond of the padres, well educated by them, and interested in meeting and talking to us.

However, some were quite run down, with padres who treated us as if we were common beggars. These missions had a much smaller number of Indians, who were shy and looked unhappy.

After leaving one such mission, I asked Miguel and Pedro if they often wished they could go back to the way things were before the Spaniards arrived.

"It is difficult not to wish for this sometimes," Miguel said. "The Chumash had a peaceful life and a beautiful place to live."

"I don't think about it, because we cannot live in the past," said Pedro. "We must forgive what happened, and move on."

"I agree, Pedro," I said. "But it's not always an easy thing to do."

After arriving back in Santa Barbara, it wasn't long before everyone around here knew about the woman and child left behind on San Nicolas Island, and the sinking of the *Peor es Nada*. The most talked about topic in Santa Barbara was whether or not the two Nicoleños were still alive—and, if they were, who might be able to rescue them.

The day after we got back, Zack left for San Pedro to tell the owner of the *Peor es Nada* the bad news, and see if there were any other ships available.

I didn't envy him at all for several reasons. To begin with, the owner of the *Peor es Nada* would be upset, and probably blame Zack for the loss of the ship.

I also wasn't optimistic he would find another one. As I already mentioned, during this time in California there were no locally owned ships. The *Peor es Nada,* as far as we knew, had been the only one.

Even if Zack did find a ship, he probably wouldn't succeed in convincing anyone to let him charter it. Even though the sinking of the *Peor es Nada* was not Zack's fault, it was a common belief that the captain and crew of a sunken ship were bad luck. It may be unfair, but when it comes to ships and the sea, people tend to be highly superstitious.

While Zack was away, Miguel, Pedro and I tried to stay busy hunting otter in the Santa Barbara area. We didn't want to go too far away in case Zack did happen to find a ship, or if one happened to come into port. However, Will told us not to be too optimistic.

"The only visitors to Santa Barbara I'm expecting are the American and British trading ships," he said. "I used to captain one of those ships, and I was always under strict orders to never deviate from the itinerary. It would take a small fortune to get a ship's captain to go anywhere but where he's been ordered to go.

"The only way you'll get back out there," he added, "is for someone in California to build or buy an ocean-going vessel, and make it available for a trip to San Nicolas. I hope it happens soon, but most likely it won't."

Zack, as we expected, returned by land, not by sea. He had no luck finding another ship, and had reached the same conclusion as Will.

There was one thing Zack wanted to tell us about his trip to San Pedro. Several times while there, he saw the one young male Nicoleño on the beach, working for a group of hunters.

"I don't know why, but everyone there calls him Black Hawk. The hunters he works for say he's the strongest and hardest-working man they've ever seen, and invariably good humored.

"However, they told me he's also quite foolish, and unable to learn how to do anything but the most basic tasks. They think whatever caused that huge scar must have affected his brain—that maybe he fell off a ledge and landed headfirst on a rock, or something like that.

"Since no one can understand the Nicoleño tongue, I guess we'll never know for sure what happened to him."

Over the next few months, people talked less and less about the woman and child on San Nicolas Island as the reality of the situation set in. There were simply no ships around, and no one knew when a vessel capable of making a trip out to San Nicolas would become available.

Some people thought the two old Nicoleños who came from San Nicolas in the canoe should risk their lives again and attempt to return to the island to save the woman and child. I don't know if Father Ramirez and the remaining Nicoleños ever considered this. We later heard the canoe was stolen, and never recovered.

It was sad to think about the unlikely series of events that caused such an unfortunate outcome. I noticed when people talked about it they always repeated a long list of things beginning with "if only."

"If only there wasn't a gale that day."

"If only those two hadn't been late."

"If only the ship hadn't been sent to San Francisco first."

"If only the *Peor es Nada's* rudder didn't break."

"If only there was another ship available."

"If only that island was not so far away."

Gradually, though, people stopped talking about it. After a few months went by, almost no one believed the woman and child were still alive, and I guess folks just don't like talking about a story with such a sad and inconclusive ending.

However, two people I met about this time still talked about it, and maintained hope that the woman and child were still alive. One was my future priest, Father Gonzalez, and the other was my future bride, Sinforosa Sanchez.

Looking back at that period of time now, I can see why people like me started to forget about the woman and child. It's hard to admit, but I had other things to think about, as did most folks here. The struggle to make a living, to build up this young town, to raise a family—these were the things that really mattered in everyday life. The lives of two Indians on a distant island, to be honest, just wasn't a cause for concern for most Santa Barbarans.

At the time, I was thirty-three-years old, and had finally found a place where I wanted to settle down, and a woman I wanted to settle down with. As Will said, there were certain things required of me to make Santa Barbara my permanent home and have a chance to convince Señorita Sanchez to become the bride of a Yankee hunter.

My new friends Zack, Miguel and Pedro had similar desires and concerns. First of all, we all needed to make a living. There was still a big demand for the skins of sea otters, so after Zack returned from San Pedro the four of us set out for a six-week otter hunt, which was quite successful.

About the time we returned, a large American trading ship came into port, looking to get rid of a load of bricks she'd been using as ballast. Zack jumped on this opportunity, and decided to build the first brick structure in Santa Barbara. He hired Miguel, Pedro and some other mission Indians to construct a two-story building. It eventually became Santa Barbara's first hotel, and is still standing. Upon finishing it, Zack sold his adobe house to me.

During this period, Miguel and Pedro both got married. They continued to live on mission land, in the houses originally built for the converts. These dwellings were small and run-down, but still the brothers were better off than most of the Indians around here. They continued to work for Zack and I, and over time became exceptionally skilled otter hunters.

I finally went to talk to Father Gonzalez about becoming a Catholic. I was worried whether he would accept me into the church if he thought my motivation was not to get closer to God, but to a woman.

As it turned out, I had nothing to worry about. Much to my surprise and relief, Father Gonzalez didn't seem to care why I came to see him. In fact, judging from the first thing he said to me, he seemed to already know.

"It doesn't matter what brought you here today. I am happy you came, and hope you find our church a comforting place to be."

I didn't realize it at the time, but I had just met the finest man I would ever know. I never saw Father Gonzalez fail to do everything he could to help those around him. He was a short, thin man with a gentle manner and a warm smile, but in a way was the most feared person in town—no one ever wanted to do anything that would disappoint such a generous and devoted priest.

He had been in Santa Barbara only about a year, but would stay for the rest of his life, and oversee the transition of the mission into a simple parish church. As the Mexican government slowly cut off his funding and took away the mission's land, Father Gonzalez never complained or lost his strong devotion to his church.

He gave me a tour of the main chapel and the mission grounds, and explained some of the rituals necessary to become a Catholic. Then, much to my surprise, he changed the subject.

"Señor Nidever, you were on the ship that left behind the woman and child on San Nicolas Island. Can I ask you a few questions regarding that?"

He wanted to know all the details of our trip to San Nicolas and the sinking of the *Peor es Nada,* and whether I thought we could find another ship. After nearly an hour of answering his questions, I asked him why he had such a strong interest in the matter.

"Señor Nidever, I do not know exactly why. As we Catholic priests love to say, God works in mysterious ways. When I think about the unlikely series of events that stranded the woman and child on that island, with no immediate hope of rescue, it makes me wonder if there isn't some reason why. And therefore I can't agree with you and the many others who think they have perished. I believe we haven't heard the ending of this story just yet."

About a week later I met Sinforosa. It happened at the wedding of a daughter of Don Jose Ortega, a ranchero and patriarch of one of the town's most prosperous families. In those days at such weddings the whole town was invited, and as it turned out I didn't need Will's help—Sinforosa simply walked up to me and introduced herself. I was somewhat tongue-tied at first, but fortunately she was not.

"I want to ask you about the woman and child left behind on San Nicolas Island. Why do you think everyone assumes they are dead?"

I remember thinking with a bit of guilt that I was fortunate the whole affair had happened, because it gave Sinforosa an interest in talking to me. Like Father Gonzalez, she asked me many questions, and believed the two Nicoleños were still alive.

"We don't know about the child," she said, "but we know the other one left behind is a woman. I'm certain she will find a way to survive until someone can rescue her. Remember, women don't give up as easily as men do."

"I don't know about that," I said. "When a man really wants something, I think you'd be amazed to see what he'll go through to get it."

If she didn't already know, I think at that point Sinforosa understood my intentions, and to my great relief encouraged me to pursue them further.

"Señor Nidever, we shall see about that. Perhaps we can discuss the matter further next Saturday. There is a birthday party for my younger sister that day at our ranch, and you are invited.

"And from now on, let's not be so formal. I will call you George, and you may call me Rosa."

Rosa.

Until that next Saturday, I could think of little else, and I was also a bit nervous. It would be my first interaction with Spanish society and Rosa's family. I was relieved that Rosa also invited Will Dana and his wife, and that week Will helped me learn the proper things to say, and when to say them.

We arrived at the Sanchez rancho, located a few miles southeast of town, at about noon. Rosa greeted us, and then introduced me to her parents and many relatives and friends. I soon found my involvement in the story of San Nicolas Island was of great interest to many at the party. In particular, Rosa's father, Don Ramon himself, told me he had given much thought to the matter, and said if there was anyway he could help get someone back out to the island to rescue the two Nicoleños, to not hesitate to ask him.

"I know it's frustrating," I told him, "but in California right now there is not a single ship available that could safely make the trip. The *Peor es Nada* was the first locally made ship, and it was poorly built and sank. The owner lost a lot of money on that venture, and I don't know if anyone will now risk so much to build another. It would require a lot of money, an experienced shipbuilder, and the right tools and materials."

"What about the trading ships?" asked Don Ramon. "If we raised enough money don't you think we could hire one of them to make a trip out there?"

"According to Captain Dana, it would take a huge number of gold coins to make that happen," I said. "San Nicolas Island is far from the normal shipping routes, and very strong currents run in between the Santa Barbara Channel and the island. The captains of those ships are not willing to take any unnecessary risks. Their business is trading, not rescuing people stranded on distant islands. Especially, to be honest, if they happen to be Indian."

Don Ramon sighed, and nodded his head. "It's true," he said. "If it was my daughter and grandchild out on that island, I would go to the ends of the earth to find another ship, and spend my last centavo to buy it. But in this case, I have to admit that all I'm willing to do for the woman and child is pray they can survive on that island for a long time."

"Perhaps they can," I replied. "Your daughter Rosa and Father Gonzalez both seemed convinced of it. And eventually the day will come when another ship visits San Nicolas, and we will finally know if they are right or wrong."

Chapter Six

A Ship Visits San Nicolas

After meeting Sinforosa, I was baptized and started going to church regularly. Will Dana sponsored me for Mexican citizenship, which I received in early 1836.

Zack, Miguel, Pedro and I continued to hunt otter up and down the coast of southern California. In between hunts, I saw Rosa often and in December received Don Ramon's permission to marry her. He agreed on the condition I first build a new house, so I purchased some land just above the beach in the southwest part of town. Zack helped me draw up the plans for a six-room adobe with a large veranda overlooking the ocean. The house was finished in April of 1836, and the wedding scheduled for June.

During this time there was very little discussion about the two Indians on San Nicolas Island. Even those who believed they were still alive, such as Rosa and Father Gonzalez, realized nothing they could do or say would change the situation—it would take a ship to do that.

Zack and I considered building a small schooner, but for several reasons never attempted it. We were doing quite well hunting otter in our canoes, which were easy to maintain and store. Then there was the cost involved—Zack had just built a new house and I was about to build one, so we would've had to borrow money to do it. Also, building a ship required certain tools and a huge load of lumber, which were hard to come by in California in those days.

Rosa and I got married that June and moved into our new house, which we still live in today. It was a happy and prosperous time for me. After all those years as a wandering hunter and trapper, I'd found this beautiful little town to settle in. I was no longer a newcomer, and married to a kind, spirited woman from a good family. I lived in one of the biggest houses in town, and was making a good living hunting otter. I was also lucky to know people here like Zack and Will, Miguel and Pedro, and Father Gonzalez. I owed much of my good fortune to their help and advice.

In particular, I was grateful to Miguel and Pedro. Because of them, I no longer felt the hatred and anger that burdened me for so long. Not to mention that Pedro saved my life.

Father Gonzalez also helped me in this regard. When I confessed to him the killing I'd done in my life, he did not judge or condemn me—instead, he patiently explained to me the need, in everyone's life, for forgiveness and redemption. God knows I've needed more than my share of both, and where I'd be without them.

Nothing else notable happened until the spring of 1837. Rosa gave birth to our first child, a son we named Jacob. A grizzly bear attacked Zack one day while we were deer hunting in the hills behind town. He probably would've been killed if I hadn't been nearby and able to shoot the bear before it did him in. His injuries were pretty severe, and he hired a local woman as his nurse, who soon became his wife. Her name was Mary Ayres, and she was born aboard an American trading vessel captained by her father. I do not recall why, but when the ship visited Santa Barbara, soon after her birth, Mary was left in the care of a local family and would spend the rest of her life here.

And finally, in May of that year, more than two years after the two Nicoleños were left behind, a ship went to San Nicolas Island. At long last, it appeared, we would learn the fate of the woman and child.

It was an American-built brig called *The Rover*, out of Boston and under the command of Captain Alexander Whitmore. *The Rover*, for many years, was based in the region of Kodiak Island, far to the north of here, and engaged in hunting and trading. The crew was mostly natives of that area, known as Kodiak Indians.

That region was also heavily hunted by the Russians and the British, so Whitmore decided to sail down south and see if he could find less competitive waters to hunt in.

He stopped in San Francisco and talked to port captain Richardson about the possibility of hunting in Mexican waters. Richardson explained that the Mexican government did not grant licenses to foreign ships, but there was one possible exception. He told Whitmore about what happened out on San Nicolas Island, and that Captain Dana in Santa Barbara may allow him to hunt there in exchange for conducting a search of the island.

And so, *The Rover* showed up in Santa Barbara about the middle of May 1837, and Captain Whitmore came ashore to speak to Will. After some discussion, the two captains came to an agreement.

The plan they settled on was for *The Rover* to spend three

weeks hunting at San Nicolas. During this time Whitmore would conduct a thorough search of the island. *The Rover* would then head to the port of San Pedro to pay the duty on their skins and reunite the woman and child, should they be found alive, with the other Nicoleños.

Will said he trusted Captain Whitmore because he'd asked for a license to hunt in Mexican territory.

"He could've gone out there to hunt without my approval, and I probably would've never known. I've heard rumors over the years that Russian ships have hunted at San Nicolas, knowing that the Mexican government would be unable to stop them even if aware of it."

Will asked Zack and me to go down and meet *The Rover* in San Pedro and make sure there were no problems between Captain Whitmore and the Mexican traders. He also wanted some of the skins brought back to Santa Barbara so the traders here would get a share of the profits.

Mainly, though, I think he wanted us there so we could get the full story of Whitmore's search for the woman and child. Whatever the outcome, everyone would want to know the concluding details of this long-running story.

We arrived in San Pedro a couple of days before *The Rover* was due back to ensure the traders were ready to transact with Whitmore, and to tell Father Ramirez that the two Nicoleños might finally be rescued.

He said he doubted the two could've survived so long. He also told us he wasn't sure what he could do for them if they were brought back alive.

"The Mexican government took almost all of the land that once belonged to the mission," he explained, "and most of our livestock. It's become difficult for me to make enough income and procure enough food to take care of the Indians who still live around the mission."

He then informed us that most of the Nicoleños were no longer around. "All three of the old men and two of the women died of dysentery. I think the change from the food they ate out on that island caused it, but we'll never know for sure.

"Some of the women left the mission to go work on a rancho. So just a few Nicoleños remain at the mission—and the one now known as Black Hawk who works for the hunters in San Pedro.

"If they find those two unfortunate souls and bring them here, I'm afraid they won't have much of a future to look forward to, but I'll do what I can."

The day *The Rover* was due to arrive we saw one of the local hunters shoot a large spotted seal from the shore. We then saw Black Hawk dive into the waves to swim out and retrieve it. The seal, which weighed at least three hundred pounds, was about a hundred yards offshore.

Retrieving such a large seal from that distance would usually require at least two if not three men, but he brought it in and hauled it up onto the beach by himself. I never saw a more impressive display of strength, and I could see why the local hunters liked having him around.

As we watched him doing this, it occurred to me that Black Hawk was likely the last living male of the Nicoleño tribe.

Finally, late in the afternoon on the day *The Rover* was due back, she appeared on the horizon. We saw Captain Whitmore get into the shoreboat, which was rowed in by four Kodiak Indians of his crew.

"They didn't find them," said Zack, just before the shoreboat reached the beach. I don't know how he knew, but moments later Whitmore confirmed it.

"Sorry to say, although the hunting was somewhat successful, our search for the two Indians was not. No sign of them at all.

"I sent a search party onto the island the day after we arrived—four of my strongest Indians. They spent two days searching and found nothing, except a few wild dogs and the remains of some huts.

"We also spent three weeks hunting in various locations around the island. If our search party somehow missed them, I have to believe they would've certainly noticed us."

I felt bad for Zack, who took the disappointing news especially hard.

"As I've always said, I should've turned back when that gale started. If I had, those two ..."

"You should stop blaming yourself," I told him. "If they hadn't been late when we were there, and if the *Peor es Nada* didn't have a faulty rudder ..."

"George," he interrupted, "thanks for trying, but I'll feel guilty about this until the day I die. Nothing you can say will ever change that."

So I let the matter drop. Then, as if we didn't feel bad enough already, we heard some news before leaving San Pedro which made us feel even worse. For some unknown reason, right about the time *The Rover* arrived in San Pedro, Black Hawk went missing. No one knew why, and he was never seen again.

So we returned to Santa Barbara and broke the bad news to Rosa and Father Gonzalez. After I told them what Captain Whitmore said, they asked me if I thought it was possible, on such a big island, that the search party could've missed them. I told them I didn't see how that could've happened, and even if it did, it's hard to imagine how anyone could've failed to notice the ship.

"The only possibility they weren't found is if for some reason they didn't want to be," I said. "And if they were still alive, after two years alone out on that island, wouldn't they want to be rescued?"

Rosa and Father Gonzalez also asked if we trusted Captain Whitmore, and I said we had no reason not to. Even so, they both refused to give up hope, and pointed out that no remains were found, which meant the two could possibly still be alive.

"Until someone I know and trust searches that island," said Father Gonzalez, "I will assume those two are alive and continue to pray for their survival."

However, as the years rolled by, the story of the stranded woman and child became almost entirely forgotten. As far as I know, after *The Rover* went to San Nicolas in 1837, no other ships visited the island for many years.

The American, British, and Russian hunting ships that used to ply the coastal waters of western America gradually stopped coming as they found more productive areas elsewhere to hunt and trade.

Even if a ship was available, people around here simply had no reason to go there. Otter were still abundant along the coast and around the other, much closer, islands. San Nicolas Island is so far away from the mainland and the other islands that it's almost as if, for a long period of time, it ceased to exist.

And so, for year after year after year, this remote island sat in total isolation—unseen, unvisited, forgotten.

I know you will find this hard to believe, but it's the truth—not until 1852, over fifteen years later, would another ship go to San Nicolas Island. She was a small schooner, slightly bigger and much better built than the *Peor es Nada*, but with the same captain and crew.

Chapter Seven

A Reason to Return

It was an eventful period of time, both for me and California. Rosa and I had three more children—George, Jr. in 1839, Marcus in 1842 and our daughter Isabel in 1846. We also started a small farm and orchard just outside of town, growing mainly grapes, apples, pears, oranges and cherries.

I continued hunting with Zack and the brothers, but as the town grew, more hunters came and the otter began to disappear from coastal waters. By about 1850, we realized that to continue making a living hunting otter, we would need a ship so we could hunt out on the Channel Islands.

At first, we had no luck. There were still no shipyards in California, and no locally owned ships available to charter. However, two things happened in California about this time to change the situation.

Both occurred in 1848. First, California became a part of the United States, although it didn't officially become a state until 1850. We saw this coming, as the Mexican government was unpopular here and never kept a large military force.

The conflict between Mexico and America over control of California was not much of a war—it was more a matter of the American forces chasing the Mexican military out of the state. This took about a year, and in early 1848 the two countries signed a treaty. In return for a payment of about eighteen million dollars, Mexico ceded California to the United States, and I was once again an American.

What really changed things in California, though, was the discovery of gold later that year in the northern part of the state. This set off a human stampede the likes of which had never been seen before.

Many gold seekers came overland by wagon, but most came by ship, and the closest port to the gold mines was San Francisco. Suddenly, there were dozens of ships in the San Francisco Bay, and some were stranded there as numerous sailors jumped ship and took off for the gold mines.

In spring of 1850, after hearing about these things, Zack and I went to San Francisco. After a few days of looking around, we met the owner of a small schooner who was willing to sell at a good price. Zack inspected the ship carefully, and after doing so said there was only one thing about it I might not like.

"Sorry, George, but this schooner is too well-built to be called the *Peor es Nada II*. So we'll have to think of a new name."

"You can call her whatever you want," I said. "All that matters to me is the ship is ours, and we can decide where she goes, and when.

"Zack, I think we're finally ready to take a trip out to Santa Cruz Island. And this time, there won't be any last-minute change in plans."

While in San Francisco, we learned some disturbing things about what was happening to Indians in northern California due to the gold rush and as a result of California becoming a part of the United States.

In short, both the new California government and the new settlers here had declared war. The goal of this war was the extermination of Indians.

I first found proof of this in a San Francisco newspaper which contained a statement from the new governor of California, a man named Peter Burnett—

"That a war of extermination will continue to be waged between the two races until the Indian race becomes extinct must be expected."

In the same newspaper I also found an account of two massacres of Indians in northern California by United States troops. One was near Clear Lake, and the other on an island in the Russian River. In both cases, it was reported that over a hundred Indians were killed.

I also heard from a gold miner I met that several new settlements were offering cash rewards for Indian scalps. Another told me of a new law which stated that anyone caught selling any kind of weapon to Indians would be hung.

Hearing all this, I couldn't help but think of how much I'd changed over the years. There was a time when I would've supported such a war. But now I felt angered by it and frustrated that I was powerless to stop it.

I also wondered why the Indians of California met such a fate. In less than a century, the Franciscans and the gold seekers had combined to completely wipe out some tribes, and send those remaining into a desperate battle for survival that continues to this day.

We decided to name our new ship *The Cora*, after Zack's mother, who died when Zack was fifteen-years-old. About a week after arriving back in Santa Barbara, we set sail for Santa Cruz Island, with a crew of six. In addition to Zack, Miguel, Pedro and I, we took my son Jacob and Pedro's oldest son Antonio.

It was nice to have the two boys on board—they were eager to learn and willing to do the hardest chores. Zack, Pedro, Miguel and I were no longer so young—Zack had just turned fifty, I wasn't much younger, and the brothers were both over forty.

We hunted at Santa Cruz Island for over a month and would've stayed longer but our little schooner was filled with otter skins. It was the most profitable hunt we'd ever done, and provided the money for a new venture that Zack and I had been planning since our trip to San Francisco.

While we were there buying our ship, we heard about the growing demand for lumber due to the increase in building caused by the gold rush. The mountains behind Santa Barbara were thick with pine trees, so we decided to build a small sawmill and began making regular runs up to San Francisco in the summer of 1851. We also continued hunting otter around the islands close to Santa Barbara—Anacapa, Santa Cruz, Santa Rosa and San Miguel.

During this period, Father Gonzalez and Rosa occasionally asked me about making a trip out to San Nicolas. I couldn't understand why they continued to think about the two Nicoleños after so many years. Everyone else had long since forgotten about them.

I had no reason at the time to go out there. I was making a good living already, and thought a trip to San Nicolas would be a waste of time and an unnecessary risk.

However, in November of 1852, a letter arrived in Santa Barbara that changed everyone's minds about going back to San Nicolas Island.

It was delivered by an American trading vessel from Boston, and addressed to Will Dana, Isaac Sparks and George Nidever. It was from Captain Whitmore of *The Rover*. Since Will was no longer port captain and I happened to be in the office that day, I saw the letter first. It read as follows:

"Dear Sirs,

"As I'm sure you'll recall, in 1837 a ship under my command, *The Rover*, visited San Nicolas Island and conducted a search for two Indians left behind there. Recently I discovered some rather disturbing information about the history of that island, and even though so many years have passed, I thought you should know about it.

"The subject of San Nicolas Island came up in a conversation I recently had with a Captain Collins, also of this port (Boston), who like me spent many years in command of a ship (*The Alert*) engaged in hunting and trading in the areas north of California. At first his recollection of what he'd heard about San Nicolas Island was hazy, but then remembered he had written about it in his log book. After searching a bit, he found the following entry in *The Alert's* log book, dated April 28, 1829:

'There is a Kodiak Indian among my crew who used to work on a Russian brig. This Indian told me about a terrible occurrence, which he says happened a few years ago on one of the islands down in the southern part of California, called San Nicolas. He said the Russian ship left about two dozen Kodiak Indians on that island, for the purpose of otter hunting. They were armed for hunting and left there for about six months.

'During this time, a dispute arose between the Kodiak Indians and the natives of the island. The Kodiaks, with their superior weapons, apparently killed most of the native men on the island before the ship returned to pick them up.'

"When I heard about this from Captain Collins," wrote Whitmore, "I decided to write this letter, and make sure you remembered that most of the crew of *The Rover* were Kodiak Indians, and that it was four Kodiaks who conducted the search of San Nicolas. It should also be noted that our ship was probably similar in appearance to the Russian brig.

"If the story Captain Collins heard is true, it is possible, perhaps even likely, that the two Indians we were searching for would've been afraid to reveal themselves to us. Judging from the size of the island and the numerous caves it has, it would not be difficult, in my opinion, for someone to hide there undetected.

"I know many years have passed since this happened, and such information may no longer be of use to you, but given the courtesy I received from you at that time, I felt it proper to share it with you. Best regards, Captain Alexander Whitmore."

After reading this, I first sent word to Zack, Miguel and Pedro, and Father Gonzalez, requesting they come to my house that afternoon. Then I went home and read the letter to Rosa.

"It's almost unbelievable," was her response. "What did the Nicoleños ever do to deserve such a fate?"

Zack arrived first, and after reading the letter just sat silently for a while, shaking his head. I knew how guilty he felt about the whole affair, and that this unexpected news would make him feel even worse. Finally, he spoke.

"Well, if it's true, it would at least solve a few mysteries. First, now we know why the old man who met you on the beach looked so frightened—he was probably worried we had more Kodiaks on board our ship.

"It would also explain why only four men remained among the Nicoleños, why Black Hawk had that huge scar on his head, and why he disappeared the day *The Rover* arrived in San Pedro. When he saw those Kodiak Indians rowing in Captain Whitmore, it probably frightened him so badly he ran as far away as he could.

"George, it looks like we're finally going to return to San Nicolas. And after we go there I'll be able to answer one more question—will I feel more guilt if we find them alive, or dead?"

Father Gonzalez arrived with Miguel and Pedro. After hearing the contents of the letter, the three of them just sat there in silence. I think the same thought was going through everyone's mind—we would have to go to San Nicolas Island and find out once and for all the fate of the two Nicoleños.

Before leaving, Father Gonzalez offered to lead us in prayer for a safe and successful journey to San Nicolas. But first, there was something he wanted to say.

"As you may know, we Catholics are big believers in saints, and that in times of need, we can pray to one of the saints to intercede with God on our behalf.

"The island which you are about to visit was named after Saint Nicholas, who lived over a thousand years ago. Over the centuries, so many miracles were attributed to the intercession of Saint Nicholas that he is sometimes referred to as Nicholas the Wonderworker.

"He also had a reputation for secretly giving gifts to those in need. Perhaps I am just a superstitious old priest, but I feel this letter is a gift, and that your trip to San Nicolas will not be a waste of time. Exactly why, I cannot say, but I suppose we'll soon find out."

Chapter Eight

Footprints

After receiving the letter, everyone was suddenly in a hurry for us to go to San Nicolas—everyone, that is, except for me.

I had to admit, Whitmore's letter was compelling. But all it really told us was that the two Nicoleños may have still been alive back in 1837. It was now fifteen years later. I felt certain going to San Nicolas would be a waste of time.

But the main reason I felt hesitant to go was the time of year. It was November—the month the storm season begins in this area. So I argued that we should wait until the following spring. My wife, priest, and friends all disagreed with me.

I remember discussing it with Rosa. She rarely gets upset about anything, but when I told her I wanted to wait until the storm season was over, she gave me a look that immediately convinced me to reconsider.

"How can you even say such a thing?" she asked in a very soft and quiet voice, which was how Rosa spoke on those rare occasions she became angry or upset. "What if it was you out on that island?"

I didn't have any better luck with the others.

"George, you know how guilty I've always felt about this," said Zack. "It's the only mistake I ever made that may have cost someone their life, and it left me with a feeling of regret I've never been able to shake.

"I haven't thought about anything else since that letter arrived, and I won't until we go to San Nicolas and finally lay this matter to rest. I can be ready to sail the day after tomorrow, and we'll want to leave very early, so don't be late."

Father Gonzalez reminded me that Saint Nicholas is also the patron saint of sailors. "I've already received his assurance," he joked, "that you will all make it back safely."

Pedro and Miguel reminded me that they were never happier than when on board *The Cora*, and couldn't wait to set sail for San Nicolas. "Besides, it will drive us crazy if we have to think about it all winter long," said Miguel.

So I didn't have much of a choice in the matter. The one thing I insisted on was that we would not take Jacob and Antonio. I refused to risk any more lives for what I considered an unnecessary trip.

And so, in mid-November of 1852, *The Cora* set sail for San Nicolas Island. Though nervous about sailing during the storm season, at least this time I knew we had a solid ship and an experienced crew.

As we sailed away from Santa Barbara, I began pondering the possibility that someone was still alive on San Nicolas Island. Surprisingly, the following thought came to me—"if you had nothing to do in life but just survive, maybe it would be possible to stay alive for seventeen years on an island."

I then realized that maybe the reason I stopped thinking about the two Nicoleños years ago was not because I thought they were dead. Perhaps it was the possibility they weren't. Maybe I didn't want to be haunted by the notion that they were still alive—and therefore still suffering the agony of loneliness, the hardship of day-to-day survival, and the constant heartbreak of searching the horizon for a rescue ship and seeing only empty ocean.

That's why Zack said he might feel even more guilt if we found them alive than if we found them dead. After all, to be alone on an island for such a long time, completely forgotten by the rest of the world—wasn't that a fate worse than death?

Anyway, I still couldn't believe anyone was alive on San Nicolas Island. Even if you had the skills and strength necessary to survive for so long, wouldn't the never-ending solitude eventually cause you to lose your mind? And once that happened, wouldn't your ability to survive also be lost?

I thought back to that day—April 10, 1835—when I saw the woman as we sailed away from San Nicolas. I still wondered why she was alone. The more I thought about it, the more convinced I became that the woman was the only living Nicoleño left behind. If I was right, it meant we were sailing out to San Nicolas Island to see if a lone woman had survived there for over seventeen years.

Well, Rosa once told me women don't give up as easily as men do, and that the woman on San Nicolas would survive until someone finally made it out there to rescue her. At long last, we would know if she was right.

On the way out I discussed some of these things with my shipmates. I asked them if they thought anyone could survive seventeen years alone on an island, without any contact with the rest of the world. They all agreed it was highly unlikely.

"Especially if you consider what the woman has been through," said Zack. "First of all, she witnessed the murder of most of the male Nicoleños by the Kodiak Indians. At about the same time, the Nicoleños were losing contact with the Indians on the other islands and the mainland, and began gradually dying out.

"And then think of that day she got left behind. Can you imagine what it was like to suddenly be alone on that island? And then all those years of wondering why no one ever came back to get her?

"Wouldn't all those things cause you to lose hope and maybe even want to die?"

For a while, no one spoke. Then Pedro made the following observation—"We can never answer such a question without knowing one thing—how strong is the woman's will to live?"

After that discussion, we didn't talk much the rest of the way. Perhaps this was because we were all a little short on sleep. We left Santa Barbara at about two o'clock in the morning so we could arrive at the island by mid-afternoon. In November the days were short, and we wanted to get to San Nicolas before dark to make sure we could anchor in a safe spot, and have some time to begin our search.

The weather was good for that time of year—a bit breezy but nothing that would prevent us from safely reaching San Nicolas. But it was November, a month in which the weather is unpredictable and can quickly change.

As we approached San Nicolas, a rather unusual feeling came over me. I've never been very sentimental, but it was something like that. I thought about how long I'd known Zack and the brothers, and all the things we'd been through together over the years. That first trip to San Nicolas seemed like a lifetime ago.

At the same time, I also began to get a feeling similar

to the one I got so many years ago as the *Peor es Nada* approached the Golden Gate—a foreboding that somehow this voyage wouldn't turn out as we hoped.

We made good time and arrived by mid-afternoon. We decided to sail around the island a bit before anchoring, in the hope we might see some sign, such as smoke from a fire, indicating the presence of a human being. We saw nothing of the sort but did notice some areas were thick with otter, and that the base of the island had many caves.

"One of those caves," Zack noted, "would make a pretty good hideout."

We eventually came to the same spot where we had anchored the *Peor es Nada* so many years before. There was still a couple of hours of daylight left and the weather remained calm, so we decided to drop anchor, head into shore and begin our search.

We wouldn't have time that day to search but a small area of the island. As I mentioned, San Nicolas is about eight miles long and three miles wide. There are numerous ridges, ravines and canyons, with not a lot of flat land. We figured it might take us several days to thoroughly search the island.

We came ashore on the same beach where we'd evacuated the Nicoleños. I don't know why we started our search in that location—if someone was still alive on San Nicolas, that person could be any number of places, and as I said it's a big island. But we had to start somewhere.

Most of the beaches on San Nicolas, including the one we landed on, are backed by steep banks of sand, which are difficult to climb. When we were there before, the Nicoleños had come down a path through one of these banks.

We could not locate such a path, so walked up the beach in search of one.

A few minutes later we found a break in the bank, and we began to walk up to higher ground. Upon reaching the top of the bank, we noticed just to the right of us a large shelving rock, from which a small spring flowed. Climbing a little closer to the spring, we saw it was trickling down onto a somewhat level area of ground about six feet below the lower edge of the rock, forming a small puddle of water.

Then, at about the same time, we all saw something that stopped us in our tracks, and made us take a few seconds to be sure we were really seeing what we thought we saw.

In the sand surrounding the puddle of water were the clear outlines of human footprints.

"Please tell me," said Zack, "you're all seeing the same thing I am."

"We don't see anything at all," said Pedro, "so you must be imagining those footprints." It was a humorous response, but we were all too shocked to laugh.

For the next several moments, the four of us just stood there staring at the footprints. I think we were all trying to think of some other possible explanation of how they could've been made. It just seemed impossible that someone had survived so long.

But the footprints were there, as plain as day. And, judging from their size, almost certainly made by a woman.

"Well, let's get moving," said Zack. "There's someone on this island who's been waiting a long time for us to return."

Above the beach we found more footprints on a trail leading uphill, but they eventually disappeared as the trail became covered with a type of moss that grows throughout the island.

About two hundred yards inland we came up to a narrow plateau, which had a good view of the eastern side of the island, and was about thirty yards in length and ten yards wide. On this plateau we found a small circular hut made of sagebrush, about five-feet tall, six feet in diameter and with a small opening on one side. There was grass growing inside of it, indicating it hadn't been occupied for quite some time.

However, just behind the hut we found four poles, about eight-feet high, stuck in the ground with chunks of seal blubber on top. We examined the blubber and found it was not yet dry, which was a sure sign someone had been to this place within the past few days.

We then walked by a stand of tall bushes called *malva real*, and in the crotch of one of these found a basket. It was covered tightly with a piece of seal skin. We looked inside and found three items—a sewing needle made of bone, a long sinew rope, and a partially completed dress or shawl made from the skin and feathers of the cormorant, which is a small, dark-green seabird. We left the basket on the ground and continued our search.

About this time the sun set and we realized it was time to return to the ship. On the way back down to the beach, the four of us looked around in every direction, hoping to spot the object of our search. But we saw nothing and soon were back on board *The Cora* preparing supper. As we ate, the last little bit of sunlight revealed a dark bank of clouds gathering on the horizon, and the wind began to pick up.

The storm, a Northwester, hit about midnight, and the ocean became far too turbulent to use the shoreboat. Once again, bad weather was preventing us from doing what we came to do at San Nicolas Island.

This time, at least, we had a different ship. *The Cora's* anchor was much heavier than the *Peor es Nada's*, and she also had a second anchor. So we dropped both of them and decided to see if we could wait out the storm.

I'm sure you can imagine how frustrated we felt. To be confined to the ship after seeing what we'd just seen was almost unbearable. And we quickly became tired of pondering questions we couldn't answer until we got back on the island and found the person who made those footprints:

Was it indeed the same woman who was left behind in 1835?

What kind of physical and mental state was she in?

Would she be happy to see us, and willing to leave the island?

Would we be able to find her if she did not want to be found?

Throughout that first day we continually checked the sky for any signs the storm was letting up. We also looked over the portion of the island we could see from the ship. Perhaps, we thought, the woman would see *The Cora*, and make some attempt to signal us. But we saw nothing, and the storm continued on.

On the second day of waiting, Zack offered to tell us a story to help relieve our boredom. I was somewhat surprised, as Zack loved to tell stories and I thought we'd heard them all by then. But after he told it, I could see why we'd never heard this one before, and why he choose to tell it at that time.

"It is a story," he began, "about being alone. It happened in the spring of 1829, when I was up in the Oregon territory trapping with the Jedediah Smith party. One day I went out hunting and was not having much luck, so I ventured out quite a distance from our camp.

"Suddenly, my horse turned and bolted, with such haste he almost threw me off. At first I didn't know what startled him, but then I looked back and saw a large black bear chasing us. It was just a few feet away, but as my horse picked up speed the bear began to fall behind. I turned back around just in time to see my horse running under the lower branches of a fir tree. I tried to duck, but the lowest branch caught me square in the forehead. Knocked me clean out of my saddle.

"When I hit the ground, I thought I was a goner. But fortunately the bear was more interested in my horse, and ran right by me. I got up and soon realized two things. One, I had no rifle or even a knife, as they were sheathed in the scabbard of my saddle, and two, the bear had given up chasing my horse and was suddenly running back towards me.

"I knew my only hope was to climb up a tree, and do it right quickly. And so I began to scurry up that fir tree, and was just out of reach of the bear when it arrived. He tried to climb up after me, but luckily the lower branches of that tree were not strong enough to hold his weight, and he slipped to the ground.

"For the next few minutes the bear was standing up with its massive forepaws on the tree trunk, looking up at me and roaring. Finally, he gave up and walked away, and sat down behind a clump of bushes at the foot of a small hill. He was still only about fifty yards from the tree and continued to watch me. Then it started to rain, lightly at first but gradually turning into a heavy downpour.

"About an hour later I saw the bear walk away over the hill, and I figured my chance to escape had come. So I lowered myself out of the tree and started walking in the opposite direction from where the bear had gone.

"It wasn't long before I realized I was lost, and because of the rain had no tracks to follow back to my camp. I also had no gun or knife to protect myself, and soon it would be dark. I wandered around for a while, trying to spot some familiar landmark that could guide me back to camp, but succeeded only in becoming more lost.

"As nightfall came, I decided the best place for me to spend the night would be up in a tree. I tore off two smaller branches and used my belt to tie them crossways to a larger branch, so I would have a place to sleep without fear of falling out.

"It was the longest night of my life, even worse than the night we sailed through the gale from San Nicolas to San Pedro. I was cold and wet and have never felt so frightened. I realized that the fear I felt wasn't because I was afraid of being killed by some animal, but because I was so totally lost and alone.

"I spent the whole night worrying I would never find my way back to camp, and get hopelessly lost. I was terrified by the possibility I would never again see another human being, and die out there alone.

"There were a few times in my life when I feared I might die. But the fear that came with being lost and alone was much worse. We all know we're going to die someday, but no one expects it to be when you are alone. I think it's the deepest, darkest fear a person can have. That night passed so slowly I thought it would never end.

"The next morning I hiked around for a few hours and

still couldn't get my bearings. I was thirsty, hungry and feeling panicked by the prospect of spending another tortuous night up in a tree.

"Then suddenly I heard the sweetest sound ever to come to my ears—someone was yelling out my name. It was a member of the Smith party out looking for me. I began yelling back and within a few minutes was rescued. I have never in my entire life been so happy to see another human being. The man who found me laughed at my joyous reaction, and then told me I looked like I'd been to hell and back.

"I suppose what we just saw out on that island brought this story to mind. I was about to go crazy after just one day of being alone. If that woman out there has really been alone for seventeen years, I'll bet anything she's no longer in her right mind. I just don't see how anyone could survive so much loneliness."

We all nodded our heads in agreement and for a while no one spoke. The silence was finally broken when Zack started coughing, and I noticed he looked a little pale.

By the end of the third day of waiting out the storm, it became clear we couldn't wait much longer. Zack was running a fever and his coughing spells were becoming more frequent. We were all beginning to suffer from seasickness due to the constant swaying and bobbing of the ship. And the storm showed no signs of letting up.

As dawn broke on the fourth day, I awoke feeling chilled, feverish and nauseous. I went up to the deck to heave, and saw Miguel there doing the same thing. He looked even worse than I felt. Then Pedro came up to tell us that Zack's fever had worsened and he looked as pale as a ghost.

The four of us didn't even have to discuss it. It was an agonizing decision to make, but we knew we couldn't risk staying even one more day. Zack felt sicker by the hour and none of us would get better until we got off the ship and to somewhere warm and dry. Fortunately, by that time Santa Barbara had a wharf, so we would be able to disembark there even if the weather stayed bad.

As we sailed away, I spotted the plateau where so many years ago I saw the woman. But this time no one was there.

Somehow I doubted we had been noticed while there. Perhaps the woman was on a different part of the island, or waiting out the storm in one of the island's caves. If she hadn't seen us, I knew she'd eventually come upon our footprints and the basket we left on the ground. Would this discovery make her sad? Hopeful? Frightened?

Once again I reminded myself that pondering questions I couldn't answer was a waste of time. And I knew there was only one question I really needed to think about—how soon could we return?

The trip back just about killed us. The rain and wind were intense, and if they had gotten any worse I don't think the four of us would've made it home. We also had to tack frequently, which lengthened the trip considerably. By the time we finally reached Santa Barbara we barely had enough strength to tie off the ship and climb down to the wharf.

Before we got back, the four of us decided to tell only Rosa and Father Gonzalez about what we'd seen. There were two reasons for this decision. One was that everyone in town would be asking questions we couldn't yet answer:

When would we be going back to the island?

How could we know if it was the same woman left

behind in 1835?

If we did find her, would she want to leave the island with us? If she did, where would we take her and who would take care of her?

The other reason was because we knew several other ship captains in the area who might be tempted to go out to San Nicolas before us, and we did not want that to happen. It was not because we cared about getting the credit for finding the woman, but rather a concern over how she might be treated after being found.

So we told everyone that due to the storm we could only spend a few hours on the island and did not see anything. But as soon as we had the chance we let Rosa and Father Gonzalez know what really happened.

They had the same reaction—even though both of them believed over the years that the woman could survive, they were stunned to learn she was apparently still alive.

Father Gonzalez bowed his head and said a prayer thanking God the woman had survived, and would finally be rescued. Rosa just shook her head and smiled as if to say, "I told you so."

Father Gonzalez then said we needed to answer some questions before returning to San Nicolas.

"Where will she live and who will take care of her? Can we find anyone who can understand her language? What about the Nicoleños you took off the island in 1835? Are any of them still alive and if so can they be found?"

"I can answer the first question," said Rosa. "If you can find her and bring her back, the woman will stay with us, and I will take care of her.

"Another question is, what will she want to do? After living on that island her whole life, will she be happy living here in Santa Barbara, especially if there's no one around who can speak her language?"

"I will do my best to find out what happened to the other Nicoleños," said Father Gonzalez. "But it may not be easy. Certainly some of them have perished by now, and those still living could be hard to find."

Rosa and Father Gonzalez asked me how long it would be before we could go back out there.

"I think we're all too tired to think about it right now," I said. "We've already tried one trip during storm season and we almost didn't make it back alive. So let's just think it over for a few days."

It was not easy, but I convinced the others that another trip to San Nicolas should wait until the following spring. It was a difficult decision, but we knew sailing to San Nicolas in the winter months was just too risky.

And so, the person who made those footprints would need to keep on surviving a little longer.

Chapter Nine

Believing the Unbelievable

That winter was unusually cold, and passed very slowly. We all tried to stay busy and avoid thinking too much about when we would return to San Nicolas. But after what we'd seen out there it was not easy.

It became difficult for me to prevent a certain image from frequently coming to mind—the sight of the woman on that plateau. Whenever I relived that moment it made me think about the thing I consider the biggest mystery of all—fate.

What is fate, exactly? Is your life somehow determined before you even live it? How much control do we have over it? Is it all in God's hands? Why do some people meet better fates than others? And why should anyone suffer a fate like that of the woman on San Nicolas Island?

Soon after our return in November, Father Gonzalez sent a letter to Father Ramirez at the San Gabriel Mission, asking if he knew whether any of the Nicoleños were still alive. We waited months for a reply, but it never came. Father Gonzalez finally decided to go to Los Angeles and see what he could find out.

"I am praying that I can find at least one of them," he said. "It will certainly cause the woman great sadness if we bring her back here and she isn't able to see any of her people."

Finally, in early May of 1853, and just a few days after Father Gonzalez left for Los Angeles, we set sail for San Nicolas Island. The six months following our trip the previous November seemed more like six years. As we left Santa Barbara, I felt a mix of two emotions—a sense of relief that at long last we were returning to the island, and a feeling of suspense—was I finally about to meet the woman I'd seen so many years ago up on that plateau?

The sky was clear and the wind mild. While we welcomed the calm weather, it made for agonizingly slow sailing. We had little to talk about to pass the time, having long since tired of useless speculation about the many potential outcomes of this trip.

We arrived mid-morning of the following day, and anchored close to the beach where we found the footprints. We started our search there, and then continued up towards the island's main ridge.

As it turned out, we did not have to go far. About an hour after beginning the search, we finally proved the unbelievable truth to ourselves, and found the person who would become known as the Lone Woman of San Nicolas Island.

We again saw fresh footprints in the ground below the spring, and then went up to where we had seen the hunks of seal blubber hanging out to dry and the basket with the feather dress. There we found nothing, which was disappointing but at least indicated someone had been there after we were.

We walked inland towards a series of small plateaus near the north end of the main ridge. One of these plateaus was the one on which I'd seen the woman.

We decided to spread out and explore separately in order to cover more territory and perhaps shorten our search. However, we stayed close enough to signal each other should one of us spot the woman.

A short time later, upon approaching the crest of the main ridge, I saw Zack giving the signal—raising his hat on his ramrod and moving it up and down. At the same time I noticed a thin column of smoke rising up from an area just beyond where Zack was.

Seeing these two things sent a rush of excitement through me. We had found the woman! I remember wishing Rosa and Father Gonzalez could be there to witness it.

Zack had followed a trail that traversed through a small canyon and led up to a large plateau. The woman was on the other side of the plateau, about fifty yards away from Zack, when he first spotted her. She was sitting cross legged next to a small hut constructed of large whale bones filled in with brush, and was in the middle of stripping the skin from a piece of seal blubber.

After Pedro, Miguel and I got to where Zack was, we decided to split up again so we would each approach the woman from a different direction. We did this because we thought it would deter the woman from trying to run away should she become frightened upon seeing us. As it turned out, such a precaution was quite unnecessary.

She saw Zack first. As he started to approach her, he noticed a pack of five dogs sitting not far behind the woman.

As he got closer they began to look in his direction and growl. But then the woman looked back at the dogs, made a loud hissing sound, and they immediately ran off. While turning back around, she looked at Zack, but did not react in any way. She merely started talking to herself and continued stripping the blubber.

A few seconds after seeing Zack she also saw the other three of us, but again showed no reaction. Because the sun was behind me from where she sat, she raised her hand to shade her eyes while looking at me, and continued talking to herself.

As the four of us got within a few yards of her, we realized the woman was not at all surprised or frightened by our presence. She had obviously seen us before we saw her, and decided we were not there to do her any harm. Then she stood up and smiled at us.

It was an extraordinary sight—one of those rare moments in life when you see something so improbable that your mind can't quite accept what your eyes are seeing. But there she was—a lone woman, still alive after eighteen years and standing right in front of us. I think we all needed a few seconds just to stare at her, so we could be sure of what we were seeing.

As for the woman, I can only guess what was going through her mind. All I can tell you for sure is she was smiling, kept talking to us, and seemed quite pleased by our arrival.

She was average height and I would guess about fifty-years-old. She had a very pretty countenance, typical of Indian women—a round face with high cheekbones, large, almond-shaped brown eyes, and a big, bright smile. Her teeth were noticeably worn down, probably from eating so much dried seal blubber. Her hair was long but somewhat matted and tangled. I assume it was originally black, but perhaps due to the many years of exposure to the harsh conditions of this island had turned a reddish-brown color.

She wore a dress made of the skin and dark-green feathers of the cormorant. The feathers were turned down and outward, and sewn together in overlapping rows so no seams could be seen. It was sleeveless, girded at the waist with a sinew cord, and almost reached her feet. When hit by sunlight the dress shimmered, making it seem like the woman was glowing.

She kept on talking as we stood there looking at her. Then she pointed at Zack and I and started laughing. I'm not sure why she laughed at us; perhaps she'd never seen a white man up close, and we looked strange to her.

She walked over to a woven sack hanging in her hut and removed from it some roots known in California as carcomite, and put them in the small fire going inside the hut. After a few moments, she removed the roots and put them on a stone platter, and placed it on the ground before us. She then motioned with her arms to indicate she wanted us to sit down and eat.

We were surprised and amused by this unexpected act of hospitality—we were worried the woman would be afraid of us, and instead she was offering us food and almost acting as if our appearance was an everyday occurrence. She continued smiling and talking away.

The place we found her was probably her main living area, judging by the large pile of ash and bones just behind her hut, and also by the many items she kept there. Nearby was more seal blubber hanging up on a sinew rope between two poles. In or around her hut were many baskets, some not yet finished, including two bottle-shaped ones lined with asphaltum that held water. These were all woven from a type of grass that grows on the island. There were also other articles such as fishhooks and sewing needles made of bone, and coils of sinew rope, which we figured she used to catch seal.

Her most valued possession was a knife made from a piece of iron hoop that was set into a wood handle. She used this knife to strip skin from seal blubber. We don't know how she came to possess the piece of iron.

During these first few minutes, though the woman was continually talking to us, we didn't say a word in response. Of course we knew she couldn't understand us even if we did speak, but I think we were simply made speechless by the mere presence of this woman. It was similar, I think, to the reaction you might have from encountering someone you thought was dead—almost like seeing a ghost. It was just a highly unbelievable sight—a woman, left alone for eighteen years on an island, not only still alive, but smiling and laughing and preparing food for us.

And so we stood there, like four human statues, staring at the woman while she continued to talk away. Finally, one of us managed to speak.

"Just imagine how long it's been," Zack said, "since she's had anyone to talk to, and enjoyed the pleasure of human company."

Since we could not understand her language, we tried to communicate by using sign language, body gestures, drawing in the dirt, and the like. It was not easy, but the woman quickly became very adept at communicating in this way.

It took several hours over the following few days to get the following information from her:

The child was killed the same day we left the woman behind as a result of being attacked by the dogs. This happened while her people were preparing to leave after our ship arrived. The child was a young boy. She used her hand to indicate how tall he was, and judging from that I would say he was about five-years-old. He apparently ran off to retrieve a fishing spear he'd left in a cave on another part of the island. When she noticed he was missing she left to look for him. We don't know for sure, but we assume the child was hers.

When she found the child he was already dead. She was able to grab his spear and chase away the dogs, but by the time she carried the body back to the village, everyone was gone.

She put the child's body inside a hut where it would be safe from the dogs, and held on to the spear for protection. She then ran off to look for the other Nicoleños. After a few minutes of searching, she came to a place where she saw our ship sailing away with her people on board. She waved her spear in the hope someone would notice and the ship would turn around and come back. She also yelled loudly but due to the howling wind could not be heard.

She chased away the dogs again, and then buried the child. After this, she became ill, and lay down in a patch of wild cabbage. For several days she ate nothing but the leaves of this cabbage but eventually regained her strength. She sang and danced and prayed and this made her feel better. She made a new hut for herself in a location from where she could see the ship if it returned.

Over the years, she saw several ships, but only one

stopped at the island. This of course was Captain Whitmore's ship *The Rover*. When she saw the Kodiak Indians from Whitmore's ship coming onto the island she became frightened, removed all signs of her existence, and hid in a cave.

She did not see our ship when we were there the previous November. Apparently she was sick at the time, and because of this and the bad weather was staying in a cave on the other side of island. After recovering from her illness she found the basket we left on the ground and saw our footprints. Upon realizing that we had already left the island she became very sad.

And so the child she buried, way back in April of 1835, was the last human being she would have contact with until we arrived in May of 1853.

She made signs indicating she wanted to know where her people were. All we could do is point toward the mainland and shrug our shoulders. She responded to this vague answer with a look of confusion, and we felt bad we couldn't give her a clear answer about the other Nicoleños. The truth is, we didn't know if any of them besides her were even still alive.

Since we'd found the woman so quickly and she obviously wasn't going to run off and hide from us, we decided to do some otter hunting before leaving. The island was thick with them and we didn't want to waste an opportunity to easily make a good amount of money. We also thought spending a few days on the island with the woman might enable us to learn a little more about her life there, and give her some time to prepare to leave.

So we tried to explain that we would all be staying on

the ship that night, and then setting up a camp on the beach the next day. I don't think she understood us, and looked confused. Finally, Zack began packing some of her things into baskets and pointed at *The Cora*, which was visible from that plateau. She seemed to finally understand at this point and began packing her things.

She had one large basket with shoulder straps so it could be carried on her back. Then she picked up two more, which she held in her arms. It was enough of a load to burden a mule, but even so she grabbed two more items before setting off with us.

One was a long stick that was partially stuck into her fire, so that one end was a live coal. No doubt she did this to ensure that if the fire went out while she was away she could easily start another one.

The other was a small basket containing the head of a seal. The brains were already putrid and oozing out. She was unwilling to part with any item of food, indicating it must have been difficult to adequately feed herself, and therefore nothing could ever be wasted.

We gathered up the rest of her possessions, and set off down a trail behind the woman, who walked at such a pace we had trouble keeping up. Despite her heavy load and walking barefoot she never slipped or stumbled.

While walking by the spring where we'd seen her footprints, she indicated to us that she wanted to stop and wash herself here, and so the rest of us walked on a bit and waited. After a few minutes she rejoined us and we resumed our walk down the beach. Upon reaching the shoreboat, we made signs for her to get in, which she did without hesitation. She crawled up to the bow and knelt down there, and put one hand on each side of the boat.

Once on the ship, we built a fire in the galley, and she seemed to like sitting next to it for the warmth. She looked perfectly content to just sit and watch us tend to our various chores, while smiling and talking away. Even though she knew we couldn't understand her, I think she was just so pleased to have someone to talk to she couldn't stop herself.

We prepared dinner, just some pork and biscuits, and handed her a plate of it. As she chewed the first few bites her eyes grew wide with wonder, and she made humming sounds to show how much she enjoyed the food. I suppose after living on seal, fish, birds, roots and berries her whole life, she found cooked meat and baked flour to be a quite a tasty change from her normal diet.

After dinner there was still some daylight left so Zack, who was pretty handy with a needle and thread, decided to make some clothes for the woman using some bed ticking. He said he wanted to preserve her feather dress and also thought she would feel more comfortable in cotton clothing.

As he began to sew, the woman watched him with great interest, as she had probably never seen a threaded needle before. She showed us one of her needles, made of bone, and displayed to us her method of sewing, which was to make a hole with the needle and then put the thread through the hole.

After watching Zack a bit she indicated a desire to help, and so we handed her an extra needle and thread and she soon got the hang of it. Before long, she and Zack completed a skirt, modified a man's shirt into a blouse and repaired an old cape of mine to make a shawl. When she came back from changing into her new clothes, she looked pleased with them and was smiling even more than usual.

We set up a cot on deck for her to sleep on. When we showed it to her and indicated this was where she would sleep, she laughed, shook her head and pointed to the island. I think she was trying to tell us that she would prefer to sleep there rather than on the ship. Anyway, due to the mild weather and the excitement of that day, I think we all rested pretty well that night.

Before turning in, we again tried to explain to her that we would be going back on shore the next day, and setting up a camp on the beach. But I think she had trouble understanding what we were trying to tell her.

What a different world it would be if we all spoke the same language. It was often frustrating and time-consuming to communicate even simple things, and sometimes difficult to tell if we fully understood one another.

However, there was one thing the woman clearly communicated to us over the next few days—she had a capacity for enjoying life that somehow had not been diminished by eighteen years of solitude. She was always laughing and in good humor, and never complained about anything.

And from then on, neither did I.

The next morning we transported all the supplies and equipment needed to set up a camp on the beach. We made tents by sticking poles in the ground and spreading sailcloth over them, using the bank as a back wall. We made one for the woman not far from our own, and brought back all of her things we carried off the day before.

While we hunted otter, the woman occupied herself by weaving baskets. She had several that were unfinished, but instead of working on one until completed she would change from one to another every so often. About midmorning she left camp for about an hour and came back with an armful of the grass she used to weave the baskets.

At lunch we made an effort to learn the woman's name and tell her ours. Her name was very hard to pronounce and she laughed at our attempts to say it. Miguel said it sounded a little similar to the Spanish name "Juana Maria" and suggested we call her that. This seemed to suit the woman just fine and so from then on that's what we called her.

Later on I noticed she had finished one of the baskets and was building a small fire. I walked over to see what she was up to and found her in the process of lining the basket in order to use it for holding water. She put several small stones about the size of walnuts into the fire. Taking the basket, which was in shape and size similar to a demijohn except the neck was much longer, she dropped a few pieces of asphaltum within it, and then added the heated stones. Soon the asphaltum started to melt, at which time she began moving the basket in a quick circular motion until the interior was completely lined. She had several of these water baskets and they never leaked, even when left in the sun.

A very amusing incident happened one day when Zack shot a female otter close to our camp. We brought it on shore to skin it, and after doing so Pedro dragged the carcass across the beach to throw it in the ocean. When Juana Maria saw this she ran up to Pedro and began vigorously protesting against such a waste of meat. She then grabbed the otter from Pedro by seizing one of its flippers, and dragged it back up onto the shore.

We realized she could probably not understand why we

kept just the skin of the animal and were throwing out the rest. We left the carcass there for a while, but after a few hours the stench became unbearable, and Zack walked over to attempt again to throw it into the ocean. This time Juana Maria did not object, and made signs indicating that the carcass smelled bad, and she did not mind us throwing it out as she liked our food better anyway.

While skinning this otter Zack noticed it was within a few days of giving birth, and before throwing it in the water, he removed the unborn one and brought it back with him. He then carefully stuffed it and gave it to Juana Maria.

"I figured since the woman is about to leave the island," he explained, "she might like this as a keepsake."

Juana Maria, upon first seeing it, began laughing as if it was the funniest thing she'd ever seen. Then, using a bit of thread, she hung the stuffed otter from the ceiling of her tent. She then sat down underneath it and tapped it with her hand to make it swing back and forth. While doing so, she again burst out in laughter.

"Maybe she hasn't had too much to laugh about the last eighteen years, and she's trying to make up for it," said Zack.

But I don't think this was the case. Juana Maria just seemed to have a natural ability to enjoy life, no matter the circumstances, and was constantly laughing and smiling.

She also seemed to get a lot of enjoyment from what you might call ordinary or everyday activities. We often saw her wandering up and down the beach gathering shells to make bracelets and necklaces. She seemed to be especially happy when weaving baskets and making jewelry, and upon finishing some item always smiled and proudly admired it for a moment before starting another.

And so, after a few days of observing her life on San Nicolas Island, I came to believe that Juana Maria survived those many years of solitude in large part by finding things to do which she enjoyed or gave her a feeling of satisfaction. I suppose she also learned to avoid thinking of all the things she did not have, or had lost in the past.

On the third day we decided to hike over to another beach we'd seen from Juana Maria's camp, and do a few hours hunting there. As we started to head out early that morning, Juana Maria indicated she wanted to accompany us, and I got the feeling there was something she wanted us to see. Before leaving she again grabbed a stick from the fire.

As it turned out, this beach was next to a part of the island that was inaccessible from the shore due to rocky cliffs and huge boulders. The island had many areas like this, all with cave openings, although we could not tell how large or small these caves were.

After a successful morning of hunting, we packed up our gear and skins to return. Just then, we noticed Juana Maria climbing up to the top of a small cliff, and beckoning us to follow her. So we decided to go see whatever it was she wanted to show us.

From the top of that cliff she led us down and around several boulders until we came to the base of another, larger cliff. In some of the fissures or cracks in the cliffs I saw some chunks of seal blubber. I figure she placed them there, out of the reach of any animal, so that she always had a store of food.

Next to this cliff was a very small beach you could not see until right upon it. At the spot where the beach met the cliff, we saw a pile of rocks. Juana Maria then began moving some of these to the side, and we soon saw they were covering a small opening to a cave. Juana Maria entered first, and made motions for us to wait outside while she first built a fire. After a few moments she came back to the entrance and motioned for us to enter.

At first, with just the little bit of light coming from the opening and the small fire Juana Maria had started, I couldn't see much. But as my eyes adjusted, I realized the cave was quite large and saw paintings on the walls of men hunting ocean creatures such as whales, dolphins and squid. They were reddish-gray in color with black outlines, and in a somewhat faded condition.

The cave was roughly circular in shape, and about twenty feet wide. The ceiling sloped up from the sides to a height of about ten feet. To the left as you entered was a crude set of steps carved into the rock, which went up to within a few feet of the ceiling. I saw Juana Maria there—she appeared to be pushing up on something, and then suddenly a shaft of light appeared. I realized the cave had a small hole in its ceiling, covered by a large flat rock. With some effort, the rock could be slid back and forth to open or close the hole.

On one side of the cave was a series of ledges and shelves built into the rock. Placed on the various shelves were many items—water baskets, smaller baskets filled with seeds and roots, fishing hooks and lines, wooden spears, knives made of bone, nets and ropes made from sinew, cooking vessels and utensils made of soapstone, a dozen or so abalone set out to dry, many small figurines or sculptures, necklaces and bracelets made of small pink shells, and another feather dress which appeared to be about half finished.

There was also a small flat area next to the fire pit covered by a thick woven mat. This must have been Juana Maria's bed and I assume this cave was her primary abode during bad weather or when she was sick.

She then took several empty baskets and began packing some of her possessions into them. I think Juana Maria knew we would soon leave the island and it might be her last visit to this cave. I wondered again what she was thinking as she gathered up her baskets and got up to leave this place where she had spent so much time. However, as we left she was, as usual, talking and laughing and smiling.

On the way back, we saw the same pack of dogs Zack encountered near Juana Maria's camp. They were about fifty feet away and in between us and the beach. As we got a little closer they started to growl at us, but then Juana Maria made a loud hissing sound and they ran away. I don't know how she so easily controlled those dogs.

After another day of hunting, we decided it was time to head home. We then tried to communicate to Juana Maria that we would be leaving the next day. I think she understood as we had already taught her the Spanish word mañana.

Soon afterwards, she walked away towards the interior of the island. Apparently, Juana Maria had some final things to do and places to visit before leaving and was gone several hours, returning just before dark. I don't know what she did or where on the island she went during that time, and again I can only guess what kind of thoughts were going through her head.

All I can say for sure is that after spending her whole life on that island, the last eighteen years of it alone, she seemed ready to go. She made some signs to us that were hard to understand, but I think expressed a willingness to leave San Nicolas because, at long last, she would see her people again.

The next morning as we prepared to leave, Juana Maria showed no signs of sadness, but was unusually quiet. I can only imagine how she felt about departing from her island home, and wondered if she knew there would be no coming back.

Just before stepping into the shoreboat, Juana Maria turned and faced the island and began to sing. She sang in a rhythm different from any I'd ever heard. The song began slow and deliberate and then increased in tempo as she went on, and then slowed down again. While singing, she also danced in rhythm to the song. We could not understand the lyrics, but I assume she was saying goodbye to San Nicolas Island, and to all of the people, her people, who had lived and died there.

The Channel Islands, home to so many Indians for so many years, were now entirely empty of them. Our task of removing the Nicoleños from San Nicolas Island was finally completed, a mere eighteen years behind schedule.

You never know what twists and turns life has in store for you. In my case, I could've never foreseen the unlikely combination of a ferocious gale, an impatient captain, and a child gone missing, and how it would bring into our lives the most unique and inspiring person we would ever know.

Just before leaving the island, I thought again about the question of fate. I wondered if Juana Maria spent much time thinking about why she ended up alone for eighteen years, and why her people were now gone from San Nicolas.

My guess is that she didn't. Maybe she knew so little about the world that she never realized what an unlucky hand life had dealt her. But I think instead she just refused to be bound by her fate to a life of sadness and despair. Perhaps Juana Maria learned what so many of us never do—that it's not only possible, but also preferable, to always see yourself as the master of your fate, rather than the victim of it.

As we sailed away, I noticed that Juana Maria never looked back at San Nicolas Island, and was instead gazing to the east, towards the mainland.

Chapter Ten

A Whole New World for Juana Maria

Soon after leaving San Nicolas the wind slowly picked up and gradually became quite strong. We figured it was the first time Juana Maria had ever been out on the open ocean, and thought she might be frightened by the heavy winds and huge swells. Instead, she responded by doing something that once again amused us all.

As the wind grew stronger, she conveyed to us by signs her intention to put a stop to it. She then knelt down, facing the direction of the wind, and prayed. She did this several times over the next hour. Then much to our surprise the wind died down until it was no more than a mild breeze.

I don't think any of us really believed that Juana Maria could control the wind, but she appeared to believe she had done so. She looked at us and smiled, as if to say, "you see, I have succeeded in stopping the wind."

"You have to admit, " said Zack, "that whatever she did seemed to work. Or, perhaps Juana Maria just played a little joke on us."

"What do you mean?" asked Pedro. "What's the joke?"

"Well, I'd bet she has a pretty keen sense about changes in the weather. After all, she's lived her whole life surrounded by ocean. So maybe she could tell the wind was about to die down, and decided to have a little laugh at our expense."

As we sailed by Santa Cruz Island, which is the largest of the Channel Islands, Juana Maria seemed fascinated by it and made signs indicating she wanted to stop there. When we shook our heads to convey to her that we would not be doing so, she looked disappointed.

Then she appeared to be asking if anyone was still living on Santa Cruz. We shook our heads and pointed to the mainland. She looked confused and must have wondered why there was no one left out there.

Once again I felt frustrated by our inability to converse with her. There is just no way to communicate certain things without words. Explaining to Juana Maria what happened to the Indians around here could only be done by someone who could speak her language.

Thus we surely hoped Father Gonzalez had succeeded in finding at least one of the other Nicoleños. How wonderful it would be for Juana Maria, after so many years alone, to see a familiar face and finally have someone to talk to.

We also felt bad we couldn't warn her about what would happen when we arrived in Santa Barbara. The news of her survival and arrival would quickly spread around town, and everyone would want to see her. Would it frighten her to suddenly be surrounded by crowds of curious strangers?

"I don't think it will bother her so much," said Pedro. "I'm more concerned about Father Gonzalez's trip to Los Angeles. I'm sure Juana Maria is expecting to see some of her people. She'll be sad if none of them are there."

As we approached Santa Barbara, Juana Maria stood

near the bow of the ship and quietly gazed at the wide expanse of land before her. It made me think back to how I felt when first seeing the ocean and the Channel Islands, and what an unreal sight that was for me. Juana Maria, after spending her entire life on an island surrounded by miles of ocean, was perhaps having a similar reaction upon seeing such a vast landscape.

As we got closer, she began to chatter away and point at the things catching her attention. At the same time, *The Cora* was sighted by those onshore, and we noticed a small crowd starting to gather on the wharf to greet us. I saw Rosa and our children, and the wives and some of the children of Zack, Miguel and Pedro. Then I noticed Father Gonzalez coming from the mission on horseback.

Juana Maria also saw this, and began laughing and pointing—it was the first time she had ever seen a horse—then placed two fingers of her right hand over the thumb of her left hand and tried to imitate the stride of the horse.

As I watched her doing this, I realized Juana Maria would have no problem adapting to her new life. She had no fear of people or things new to her. Instead, her reaction was one of amusement and curiosity.

As *The Cora* pulled up to the wharf, I looked at Rosa and Father Gonzalez, and they were both grinning like fools. I couldn't blame them for being so happy. After all, they were the only two people who truly believed through all those years that the woman was still alive.

Among the group gathered there were my son George and his friend Nick, who were often together. When the two of them saw the woman on board, they called out to us—"Did you find the Indian woman? Is that really her?"

When I nodded my head, the two boys immediately

turned and began running towards town—they obviously wanted to start spreading the news that the woman had been found and brought back. But I yelled at them to stop and wait.

"I don't want the whole town coming here before we can unload the ship and get the woman ashore," I told them. "Word will get around soon enough, believe me."

The boys were disappointed, but I think they understood. Even at their age they knew what a unique and compelling story this was, and that everyone would want to see the woman. It was nothing short of the most sensational event in the history of Santa Barbara.

When Juana Maria stepped off the ship and onto the wharf, the first people to greet her were Rosa and Father Gonzalez. Both spoke to her some words of welcome and, even though she could not understand them, she smiled graciously and seemed to comprehend somehow what they were saying.

What made her smile the most were all the children gathered there on the wharf. Besides George and Nick, my son Marcus, who was then about ten years old, and my daughter Isabel, then about seven years old, were also there, as well as two of Miguel's children, two of Pedro's and one of Zack's.

Before leaving the wharf, Juana Maria insisted on giving gifts to all the children. She removed from one of her baskets some shell necklaces, which she gave to the girls, and some knives made of bone for the boys. She appeared to enjoy handing these out even more than the children enjoyed receiving them.

I could sense, however, her disappointment that none of her people were there to meet her—Father Gonzalez had apparently been unable to find any of the other Nicoleños. She kept looking around as if expecting to see someone. At one point she turned to Miguel and Pedro and through signs appeared to ask "where are my people?" All they could do in response was shake their heads and shrug their shoulders.

However, she started smiling and laughing again upon seeing, at the foot of the wharf, my son Jacob with his oxcart and horse. I thought she might be afraid of such large animals, but it was just the opposite. She walked right up to the horse and began petting it, and then closely examined the ox. Zack's wife Mary had some apples with her and gave one to Juana Maria to feed to the horse. This she did without hesitation and was delighted when the horse ate the apple from her hand.

As we watched all this, I told Rosa and Father Gonzalez how relaxed and friendly Juana Maria was when we first found her. "We all thought she might try to run away from us, or that it would at least take some time for her to learn to trust us. But when we first approached her, she just stood up and smiled, and then started cooking some roots for us."

Then I told them about what happened on April 10, 1835—how the child went missing and was killed by the dogs, causing Juana Maria to be left behind.

"I always had faith," Rosa said, "that the woman could survive. But after all she's been through, it's amazing she's still so full of grace, and full of life."

"I agree," said Father Gonzalez. "I thought she would be angry or withdrawn, and afraid of everyone and everything. But instead, I see a woman who's gracious, generous, and already friends with the first horse she's ever seen!"

After we finished loading up the oxcart with Juana Maria's possessions and some things of mine from the ship, we began to head down the road that skirts the southern part of town and leads to our house. As we did so, many people approached us to ask about the woman.

"Are you sure? This is really the same woman left behind all those years ago?"

I enjoyed watching the reaction when I told them Juana Maria was indeed that woman. Many responded as if witnessing a true miracle. Jaws dropped, eyes widened and heads shook back and forth in disbelief. Some refused to believe it until assured by Father Gonzalez that I was telling the truth.

Everyone wanted to have a closer look at Juana Maria, shake her hand and look at her things in the back of the oxcart. I thought all the attention might bother Juana Maria, but this didn't happen. She seemed to understand why people were so interested in her, and was friendly and gracious to everyone who approached her.

We soon had about fifty people gathered around us. I started to get a little upset by this, but then recalled my own reaction when I first saw Juana Maria. It was such an unbelievable sight I had to stare at her for a while to really believe it. So I couldn't really blame anyone for wanting to have a good look at her. Furthermore, she didn't seem to mind the large crowd of curious onlookers.

"Haven't you always wondered," joked Rosa, "what it would be like to have everyone in town visit our house at the same time?"

"I don't see how we can avoid it," I responded. "But I'm worried it'll be too much excitement for Juana Maria. I think we should tell everyone to come back tomorrow so she can have a little time to get used to her new home."

Father Gonzalez agreed. As we approached our house, followed by an ever-growing crowd, he offered to announce to everyone that they would need to wait until the next day to see the woman.

At that point, however, we looked over at Juana Maria and she was clearly enjoying herself. Then I saw my daughter Isabel walk up to her and take her hand. This really surprised me, as Isabel was usually shy around strangers. But for some reason, she felt very comfortable around Juana Maria, and the two of them walked along together as if they were old friends.

And so we decided, come what may, to let the people stay and see how Juana Maria would react to it all. So far it looked like she didn't mind all the attention. Perhaps after so many years of being alone she was happy to be surrounded by so many people.

However, I could still sense her disappointment that none of her people were there. She continued to look around as if searching the crowd for someone she knew. I don't know for sure, but I think Juana Maria was beginning to realize that she was in a different place than the one her people were taken to so many years before.

I asked Father Gonzalez about his trip to the Los Angeles, and he shook his head and frowned.

"It did not go well at all, I'm sorry to say. There are no Nicoleños remaining at the San Gabriel Mission—they have either already died or left to go work on one of the ranchos. So the only hope of finding any of them is to make inquiries at the ranchos in that region. That could be quite a long and difficult undertaking.

"Only one hopeful thing happened at San Gabriel. I

found out from the padres that among the Indians still living around the mission, there are several different languages spoken. It's possible one of those languages is related to the Nicoleño language, so I arranged for some of the Indians there to come to Santa Barbara and see if they can communicate with Juana Maria. It is not much of a hope, but it was all I could do.

"In the meantime, let's pray she can cope with living in a world where no one speaks her language. It's almost too sad to think about—she finally gets rescued after spending all those years alone, and yet she still has no one to talk to."

As we arrived at our house, the crowd of people was quickly growing. By the time we finished unloading everything from the cart, there were about 150 people waiting around the perimeter of our house, hoping to get a closer look at Juana Maria.

We took her inside to put away her things and show her where she would be staying. Rosa had converted a small room at the back of the house into an extra bedroom by adding a cot and a dressing table. We put some of her things into the room and tried to make her understand it was where she would sleep. Juana Maria laughed and shook her head in disbelief. She ran her fingers along the smooth adobe walls and stared up at the ceiling and touched all the furniture.

Again, I wish I could've known what was going through her mind. After spending her entire life on San Nicolas Island, living in brush huts and dark caves, it must have been quite unreal to be surrounded by walls, ceilings, windows, doors, wooden floors, furniture and wax candles. And also, of course, other people.

During those first few minutes in our house, she just

walked around the various rooms gazing at the things she was seeing for the first time. Rosa and our four children were also inside the house, and I think she readily understood that Rosa was my wife, the children were ours, and she would be living here with my family.

About this time some of those in the ever-growing crowd surrounding our house came to the door and asked if we could bring Juana Maria outside so everyone could see her. We were a little hesitant, worried that being surrounded by so many strangers would cause her to feel uneasy or frightened. We looked at Juana Maria, who was gazing out of our front window at all the people gathered there. Then she once again did something that surprised us all.

She motioned for us to wait, and then went into her room. Moments later, she came out wearing her feather dress, and indicated she wanted to go outside and show it to everyone.

Juana Maria went out through the front door onto the veranda, which is about three feet above ground level. As everyone noticed her, a noise came forth from the crowd—a combination of clapping, shouting and whistling. It was akin to what you hear in a playhouse when an audience cheers an actor at the end of a great performance. The motive, I'm sure, was the same—to show appreciation for providing something thrilling and memorable. Juana Maria's heroic feat of survival clearly touched people in a way that could never be matched.

The response from the crowd did not affect Juana Maria. She merely smiled, stepped to the edge of the veranda so everyone could see her, and began to sing.

It was the same song she sang when leaving the island. Then she began to dance as well. The movements of her dance were slow and in rhythm with the song. At the same time, the sun was shining on her feather dress so it glowed with a dark green color.

It was quite a scene. About half the people in town were there, with more showing up by the minute. They were all entranced by this unbelievable sight—the long-forgotten woman of San Nicolas Island, left behind and assumed to be dead for eighteen years, but still alive and now singing and dancing on the front veranda of the Nidever family home.

After finishing her song, the people began cheering and whistling again. Then the crowd slowly surged forward. Some were just trying to get a closer look at Juana Maria and her shimmering feather dress. Others bore gifts such as blankets, clothing, jewelry and baskets of fruit or bread, and stepped up onto the veranda to give them to Juana Maria. Upon receiving each gift, she carefully put it aside and then thanked the person giving it by smiling and bowing her head. Many of these gifts were presented by children, who seemed especially drawn to her, and less shy about approaching and trying to talk to her. She clearly enjoyed having the children around her much more than receiving the gifts.

This continued on for some time, and although Juana Maria didn't seem to mind all the attention, it was getting dark and well past our normal suppertime. And so I stepped out front and began asking people to leave, promising that they would be able see the woman again.

By the time everyone finally left, it was almost dark and Rosa was busy preparing dinner. Juana Maria changed into a dress and sweater that Rosa had given her, which were much nicer than the clothes we made for her out at San

Nicolas. She came out of her room laughing and with a big smile on her face. She clearly liked her new clothing, and was also curious about it. She kept running her hands over the sweater, made of wool, no doubt wondering how such a material was made and where it came from.

We then ate supper, which was quite an experience for our new guest. Rosa that night served beef and potato stew with freshly baked bread. Juana Maria's delight at tasting such food for the first time was humorous to watch.

Upon taking her first bite of the stew, she made a loud humming sound, indicating she thought it was quite delicious. We then showed her how to dip the bread into the stew and then her humming grew even louder. My family and I were amused to see someone showing so much delight from eating food which was common fare for us.

What really delighted Juana Maria was the fruit we served after dinner. Someone had given her a gift of strawberries, apples and oranges and upon trying each one her face showed an expression indicating she had just eaten the most delicious food ever. After eating several strawberries and a slice of orange and apple, she leaned back in her chair, rubbed her hands over her stomach and made a loud moaning sound of satisfaction.

This made Isabel laugh. She of course couldn't comprehend that Juana Maria had never tasted such food before.

"Why is she acting so funny," she asked, "just from eating some stew and some fruit."

"Well," said Rosa, "it's because she's never eaten stew or fruit before."

"Why not?"

"Because she's lived her whole life on an island where the only things to eat are fish and abalone and seal meat and things like that."

This answer caused Isabel to look a little sad for a moment. Then she looked up at Juana Maria, who was sitting next to her, smiled and took her hand. Then she put her other hand on her stomach and made a similar moaning sound of satisfaction. This gave us all a good chuckle, and I could see again that for some reason Isabel was fond of Juana Maria and liked to be near her.

After supper, Rosa wanted to give Juana Maria a bath, and asked the boys to retrieve a few buckets of water from the well, heat them up on the cookstove and pour them into our bathtub.

"What a day it's been for Juana Maria," said Rosa. "For the first time in her life she set foot on the mainland, saw a horse, ate some beef stew and fruit, and was inside a real house. In between all that she also sang and danced for half the town of Santa Barbara.

"So I figure it might be a good time for one more thing she's probably never experienced before—a hot bath."

Just before we completed the task of filling up the bathtub, a knock came on our door. I opened it and saw standing there a man named Jim Trussel, the captain of a schooner based here in Santa Barbara who transported dry goods up and down the coast. He was someone I never much cared for, as he had a well-deserved reputation for holding on to goods until they were scarce, and then charging a higher price. I also had a pretty good idea of why he came to our house.

"What can I do for you, Captain Trussel?" I asked.

"Well, Captain Nidever, I have a business proposal you might be interested in. These days I spend a lot of time in San Francisco. You know what a big town it's become since the gold rush and, well, when I was here earlier watching the woman sing and dance, I couldn't help but think of how many people up there would pay to see it—"

I interrupted him before he could say anything more.

"Captain Trussel," I said, "the woman is in the care of my wife. So instead of asking me, I think you should talk to Rosa."

At this point, I think Trussel realized he'd made a mistake, and started making excuses to leave. But I grabbed him by the arm and held him inside the door while I called Rosa over.

"Rosa," I said, "Captain Trussel here says he'd like to take Juana Maria to San Francisco and put her on exhibition. Says we could make a lot money."

"Well," said Rosa, "what an interesting idea. But I think I have an even better one."

She then walked over to the cabinet where I keep my guns. She removed a rifle and pointed it straight at Trussel, who began struggling to escape my grip as Rosa spoke to him in that very soft voice she used only when really angry.

"I think instead, Captain Trussel, you should go to San Francisco alone, and put yourself on exhibit. People will surely pay good money to see a man who has no rear end to sit down on!"

That was last we ever saw of Captain Trussel. It was because of people like him we did not want word getting out the previous November about what we'd seen on San Nicolas.

After that, Rosa took Juana Maria into the small room we use for bathing and washing clothes. They came out about twenty minutes later, and I could see our guest had very much enjoyed her hot bath. Then Rosa sat her down on a chair and brushed her hair.

While doing this, Rosa handed one of her most treasured possessions to Juana Maria—a silver-backed hand mirror. Juana Maria held it up to her face and laughed upon seeing her own clear reflection. "Now she, too," said Rosa, "can see the long-lost woman of San Nicolas Island."

Well, it had been quite a day—for my family, for the little town of Santa Barbara, and especially for Juana Maria, who looked very relaxed as my wife brushed her hair. It had all gone well so far, but I was already worried about how Juana Maria would adapt to her new life.

While she clearly enjoyed all the attention and being around my family, I knew if we couldn't find any of her people it would cause her immense disappointment. I also wondered if she could be happy living in a place where no one spoke her language, and was so totally different from where she had come from.

Chapter Eleven

The Last Nicoleño?

Throughout the next day a steady stream of visitors came to our house to see Juana Maria. I would guess over two hundred people came, including many who'd already seen her the day before.

I know of only two other comparable events in the history of Santa Barbara. In 1840, California's first bishop, Diego Garcia, visited here and the whole town gathered to celebrate the event. Guns and cannons were fired from the presidio, and the chapel bells rang as a gilded carriage conveyed the bishop to the mission.

In 1847, near the end of the battle for California between America and Mexico, Commodore Stockton arrived here and everyone gathered to watch him raise the American flag over Santa Barbara.

But neither of these events matched the excitement caused by the arrival of a lone Indian woman who could not even converse with anyone. I have to admit, even though I despised Captain Trussel for suggesting we put Juana Maria on exhibit, there is no doubt that people were captivated by her remarkable feat of survival, and would've paid to see her.

For weeks after Juana Maria's arrival, people continued to show up at our house. Some of them came from miles away. Word even spread to passengers of the ships that stopped here during that time. The captain of *The Fremont*, one of these ships, offered me a thousand dollars for her. I politely explained to him what happened when Captain Trussel made such an offer.

Despite the constant flow of visitors, Juana Maria appeared to be happy with her new life. She especially enjoyed being around children.

Many people came bearing gifts, which Juana Maria graciously accepted. However, as soon as they departed, she would offer the gifts to my children, or sometimes to Rosa, and wait to see their reaction. We soon realized all the things she received were worth nothing to her, except the happiness she felt when passing them on to others.

On the second day, Juana Maria again used signs and gestures to ask us about the whereabouts of her people. Our inability to explain the situation to her was frustrating, so I asked Father Gonzalez to think of a way to give Juana Maria at least some idea of what had happened to the other Nicoleños.

The next day, he brought a map of the southern California area, and a drawing of an island with a ship in the foreground and many Indians on it—representing the Nicoleños who left on the *Peor es Nada*. Using this and the map, Father Gonzalez tried to show Juana Maria that the other Nicoleños were taken to the mission in San Gabriel. Then he tried to explain that some of them had died, and the rest had left the mission and now could not be located.

Juana Maria looked confused. I think she understood some of Father Gonzalez' attempted explanation, but perhaps couldn't comprehend that she now lived in a place where it was difficult to find people, especially Indians, unless you knew exactly where they were.

THE LAST NICOLEÑO?

She then appeared to ask Father Gonzalez if he would try to find her people, and he nodded his head. However, he did so with a rather skeptical look on his face, as if telling Juana Maria he did not expect to find them.

A few days later, the Indians from the San Gabriel Mission who Father Gonzalez had spoken of arrived in Santa Barbara. There were four of them, three men and one woman, who came from different tribes in the southern California area. We hoped at least one of them spoke a language related to the Nicoleño tongue, and would be able to communicate with Juana Maria.

We took her to the mission, where she attempted to speak with the four Indians. After a few minutes of trying, it became clear that none of them could converse with her.

"I'm disappointed, but not surprised," said Father Gonzalez. "During the mission era, the padres learned there are many different Indian tribes in California, each with its own language. We'll never know for sure, but it's possible the Nicoleño language was only spoken on San Nicolas Island."

As we walked back from the mission, many people joined us to get a closer look at Juana Maria or to give her a present. I was worried that the unsuccessful meeting with the Indians would cause her to feel sad and disappointed, but as always she smiled and was friendly to everyone who approached her.

We felt great sympathy for Juana Maria. It must have been extremely frustrating to be so limited in her communications with others. She couldn't have a real conversation with anyone, nor express her thoughts and get detailed answers to the many questions she had.

Because of our inability to communicate with her, we

could not explain why we didn't know where the other Nicoleños were, or if any of them were even still alive. There was no way for her to know that they entered a vastly different world after leaving San Nicolas Island—a world where Indians often didn't survive very long.

Despite being alone, Juana Maria had a much better chance of surviving those eighteen years than did the rest of her people. She was free from the diseases that ravaged Indians here, had enough to eat, and was never surrounded by people who tended to view you as less than human.

A few days later, Father Gonzalez, Zack, Miguel, Pedro and I left on horseback for Los Angeles to see if we could find out anything about the Nicoleños. We had no clear idea of where we should search—we knew if any of the Nicoleños were still alive, there was no telling exactly where they might be.

All we knew is that some of the Nicoleños had already died, and the rest left the San Gabriel Mission to go work at a rancho. But we didn't know which rancho, and there were dozens of them in the Los Angeles area.

If Father Ramirez had known that the woman would survive and eventually be rescued, perhaps he would've tried to keep track of the Nicoleños. But like most of us he assumed, after *The Rover* searched San Nicolas back in 1837, there was no one still alive out there.

Upon arriving in Los Angeles, we stopped to see Father Ramirez to tell him we'd come to search for the Nicoleños. We were surprised to learn he'd found some information that might help us.

"Just last week," he said, "I was cleaning up and organizing our rectory, and came across some old records kept by a missionary named Father Gallegos, who served here for over forty years. He was already quite old when I arrived here in 1831, but lived until 1845.

"As you may know, the missions in the early days kept records about all the Indians who lived there—their names, age, and the dates of their baptism, marriage and death. But starting around 1825, when the Mexican government took over control of the missions, and the population of Indians was decreasing, the padres gradually stopped keeping such records.

"However, Father Gallegos continued to do so, and it appears he took a special interest in the Nicoleños, as he recorded information about all fifteen of them."

Father Ramirez then showed us these records. By the time of Father Gallegos's death in 1845, twelve of the fifteen Nicoleños were listed as deceased, including the one young male known as Black Hawk, who disappeared in 1837 and was never seen again. The cause of death for the other eleven was listed as dysentery.

So there were just three Nicoleños possibly still living, all women. According to the records, those three had left the mission to go work on a rancho. One was named Maria Elena, who left in 1839 to work at the Dominguez Rancho, located ten miles east of Los Angeles. The other two, named Juliana Maria and Juanita Francisca, both left in 1842 to work at the Valencia Rancho, which is ten miles north of the Dominguez Rancho.

Father Ramirez told us he still remembered Juliana Maria and Juanita Francisca. While at the mission, they were always together and speaking to each other in the Nicoleño tongue. He believed them to be sisters, as they looked very much alike, and also the youngest Nicoleños—only about twenty-years-old when brought to the mission.

The last thing Father Gallegos wrote down about the Nicoleños was this: "They missed their island existence, and many of them expressed a desire to return there. The sadness resulting from the separation from their island home, and gradually from each other, may have been responsible for their deaths. Many of them seemed to simply lose the will to live."

We went first to the Dominguez Rancho, and located the owner. I asked him if there was an Indian woman named Maria Elena working there. Before responding, he scowled at Miguel and Pedro and gave them a dirty look.

"Why do you care," he said, still sneering at Miguel and Pedro, "about some peon Indian woman?"

"If you know her," said Father Gonzalez, "please tell us where we might find her. It is of great importance to us."

"Great importance, huh? Padre, don't you know by now that nothing about an Indian could be of great importance?"

Then he looked at Zack and me. "You've already wasted enough of my time. So take your pious old padre and your two worthless peons and get the hell off my ranch."

This man, unfortunately, was somewhat typical of those in his position. It was obvious he wasn't going to help us. Unless, that is, he was forced to.

I felt a sudden surge of anger. I looked at Miguel and Pedro, who were my friends. Then I thought of Juana Maria, and how much it would mean to her to see another Nicoleño.

I decided I wouldn't accept such treatment, or leave the ranch until we had an answer to our question. So, as the owner turned his horse to ride away from us, I grabbed my trusty Hawken rifle, aimed it and fired. As always, the bullet went exactly where I wanted it.

At the same instant, the owner's hat flew off his head, and his horse, startled by the rifle shot, reared up and dumped its rider onto the ground. I quickly reloaded, got off my horse, and walked over to him. As he tried to stand up I gave him a swift kick in the ribs, knocking him back down. Then I picked up his hat, stuck it back on his head, and pointed my rifle at him.

"Señor, my friends here will now search your ranch for the person we are looking for. If you try to stop them, I'm going to shoot your hat again, and this time my aim might not be so accurate."

And so the others went off in search of Maria Elena, while I stayed behind to make sure the owner caused no further problems. I kept my rifle trained on him so he dared not move, but that didn't stop him from yelling a string of curses at me. He also demanded to know why it was so important to us to find this Indian woman.

At first I was inclined to just tell him it was none of his business, but then for some reason I went ahead and told him the whole story of the Nicoleños and Juana Maria. After doing so, I was somehow not surprised to see a change in the owner's behavior.

"Señor," he said, "I thought you came to my ranch to cause some kind of problem. I now see you came only to help this poor woman. You and your friends must accept my apology."

It was the first time, but not the last, I saw Juana Maria's story have such an effect on someone.

"I am also sorry to say I believe I remember the woman you seek. She was not here very long before she died. If I recall correctly, it was consumption."

A few minutes later, the others returned to tell me they found an old Indian ranch hand who remembered Maria Elena. His recollection of her confirmed what the owner told me.

We received a much nicer welcome at the Valencia Rancho, our last hope for finding one of Juana Maria's people. The owner there greeted us graciously, and we explained the reason for our coming. What he told us in response was heartbreaking.

"The two women you seek worked here for many years. Juliana and Juanita were wonderful servants and worked very hard for us. But about a year ago, Juliana became sick with consumption and died. Juanita was despondent and seemed to lose her will to live. She stopped eating and taking care of herself. I am not sure exactly what killed her, but she died just a few weeks later."

I've never felt as sorry for someone as I did for Juana Maria at that moment. She was indeed the last Nicoleño. There would be no joyful reunion, and no one to speak to in her own language.

There was nothing more to do except return to Santa Barbara, deliver the sad news to Juana Maria, and do our best to explain the sad fate of her people.

When we arrived back at my house, Juana Maria was sitting with Rosa on the veranda. I think she knew just from looking at us that our search was unsuccessful. Then Father Gonzalez walked over and knelt down in front of her. He took her hand, looked in her eyes, and shook his head back and forth.

Juana Maria smiled and nodded, as if to say, "I understand you did not find any of my people, but thank you for trying." She then turned her chair toward the ocean and just sat there silently, looking to the west for a very long time.

Over the next few days Juana Maria seemed to be content. People still came to see her at my house, and she continued to be friendly and gracious. She enjoyed walking into town with Rosa and Isabel, and always returned with some kind of gift, usually fruit or some jewelry, which she passed on to the children.

She also liked to take long walks on the beach, and watch the arrival or departure of the ships that came here. I will never know for sure, but I think she was happy just to be in a place where there were always other people around.

However, not long after our return from Los Angeles, Juana Maria's behavior began to change. The first sign of this was a loss of appetite. We thought maybe she was having problems with her stomach, perhaps due to all the different foods she was eating for the first time. Rosa made an effort to provide food for her, such as fish, abalone and seal, similar to what she lived on at San Nicolas. Juana Maria politely thanked her for doing so, but showed no desire to eat such things.

Up until this time, we had been trying to teach Spanish to Juana Maria, in the hope she might eventually be able to better communicate with us. She was a quick learner, and memorized many words and names. But about the same time we noticed her loss of appetite, she lost interest in learning any more Spanish.

Then she stopped taking walks on the beach or in to town. Instead, she seemed content to just sit in a rocking chair on the veranda, and spend hours looking out at the ocean and quietly singing to herself. People still came to see her occasionally, and while she was always friendly and courteous, she no longer sang and danced or put on the feather dress.

We were all quite concerned and couldn't figure out what was wrong with her. She was eating very little, and no longer desired to do anything but sit on the veranda in the rocking chair. Slowly but surely, she was getting physically weaker.

Finally we asked our friend Dr. Brinkerhoff, the most highly regarded doctor in Santa Barbara at that time, to come over to our house and examine Juana Maria. After doing so, Dr. Brinkerhoff shook his head and said he couldn't see anything obviously wrong with her.

"It's quite mysterious," he said. "There is no evidence of any disease or illness which would cause a loss in appetite or prevent her from being physically active. Frankly, I'm at a loss to explain what's ailing her."

At that point, we knew only one other person who might be able to help Juana Maria—an Indian medicine woman named Luisa Tumamait. She was one of the few Chumash still practicing the traditional ways of healing, and was highly respected by the local Indians.

She came the next day. I'm not sure exactly how she did it, but Luisa figured out what was wrong with Juana Maria, and that the problem was likely incurable.

Luisa Tumamait was from one of the few Chumash families still using an Indian surname. She was getting on in years but her eyes were clear and bright and she walked briskly. Her clothes were similar to most Indian women, but she wore a necklace which held several eagle talons and bear claws. She also carried a woven sack containing items such as sage, elderberry, and willow bark, which she used for healing various ailments.

Luisa sat down next to Juana Maria and held her hand while humming softly. She put her ear near Juana Maria's face, as if to listen to her breath, and then spent a few moments looking into her eyes. She then started singing and chanting in the Chumash language, which went on for quite a while. While Luisa did this Juana Maria closed her eyes and looked very relaxed.

After she finished the singing and chanting, Luisa closed her eyes and took several slow, deep breaths. Then she turned to us and spoke.

"Please do not feel bad, because it is not your fault, but Juana Maria will not survive here much longer. Her body is weakening because her spirit is preparing to leave.

"It may be difficult for you to understand, but I will try to explain. Juana Maria, until she came to Santa Barbara, lived her whole life as an Indian on San Nicolas Island. Never mind that she spent much of her life alone, it does not matter. She was a true Indian, living in the traditional Indian way.

"Until the white man came and forced us to change, Indians had a much different way of life and view of the world. We didn't see ourselves as the most important thing in this world. All that mattered was living in harmony with all that was around us. We always believed we were a part of the world of plants, animals, rivers and oceans—not separate from it.

"That is why Indians never attacked the mountains and rivers to get gold. It is why we never bought or sold our land for money. And it is why we are still struggling to adapt to the white man's world.

"The Indians around here, for many years now, have been learning to survive in the white man's world. But not Juana Maria. The Indian way of life is all she knows.

"Now she is in Santa Barbara, which is not a place where she can continue to live the way she always has. Even though everyone is treating her kindly, and she is happy to no longer be alone, she will never be able to adapt to living here.

"The reason Juana Maria decided to leave the island was that she thought her people were still alive, and in a place where they could still live an Indian way of life. Instead, her people are gone, and so is the world they once lived in. Now that she has realized this, there is no reason or purpose for her to continue living here.

"There is only one cure for her—to return to San Nicolas Island and be reunited with her people there. And it is not possible to do that.

"There is nothing we can do. Her body and spirit are drifting away from this world, and soon she will be gone."

It was the strangest and saddest thing we ever experienced.

The sad part was watching Juana Maria grow weaker by the day and be helpless to do anything about it. We all did what we could to make her comfortable and keep her company. Isabel spent many hours sitting next to her on the veranda, holding her hand and singing to her some children's songs she knew. Father Gonzalez was a frequent visitor, as were Zack, Miguel and Pedro and their wives.

However, I sometimes wondered if our efforts to keep

her company only made her feel even lonelier. After thinking about what Luisa told us, I realized Juana Maria was still very much alone in the world. Yes, there were people around her now, but not her people. We couldn't speak her language or ever know what it was like to be an Indian on San Nicolas Island.

The strange thing was that Juana Maria herself never appeared to be sad. She continued to smile and be cheerful even though her body was getting weaker and thinner by the day. I will never know for sure, but I think that Juana Maria, during all those years alone on San Nicolas Island, somehow developed a capacity for happiness so powerful it could not be stopped by any earthly event—including the coming of her own death.

It came early in the morning of a sunny summer day. Rosa went in to check on Juana Maria and found her unconscious and breathing very slowly. Rosa took her hand and called her name softly to see if she would awaken. She finally did, but just long enough to smile and point upwards with her other hand. We will never know for sure, but we think she was trying to tell us she was happy, for she would now see her people again. Then she released Rosa's hand and took her last breath.

Juana Maria survived eighteen years alone on San Nicolas Island. But after just seven weeks in Santa Barbara, she was gone.

I sent my son Jacob into town to tell everyone the news. Father Gonzalez arrived and told us he would hold a funeral for Juana Maria the next day. I told him I would make a coffin, and requested he come back later with a funeral carriage to take her to the mission.

I went out to our woodshed and sawed the boards with which I made her coffin. As I started to put it together, I thought about what Luisa had told us about the world of Indians. Many questions came to mind.

Why were Indians and whites so different? Why was I raised to believe that Indians were my enemy? Would I ever be able to completely forgive myself for the killing I had done? And why was the death of an Indian woman I knew for such a short period of time causing me to feel such deep remorse and regret?

After finishing the coffin, I took a chisel and an awl and carved the figure of a whale on one side of it, and the figure of a cormorant on the other. Then I carried Juana Maria's body outside, placed it in the coffin, nailed down the lid, and waited for Father Gonzalez to arrive with the funeral carriage.

Final Chapter

For as Long as Stories Are Told

Looking around at the large crowd gathered for Juana Maria's funeral, I thought of how unprecedented it was for so many people to come pay their respects to someone they hardly knew, and who'd lived here for such a short time.

Father Gonzalez began by talking about Juana Maria's life, or at least what we knew of it.

"It's the most inspiring life story you will ever hear. I want everyone to take a moment to think about it. Try to imagine being alone and forgotten by the rest of the world for eighteen years. Would you be able to survive such a thing?

"Some say it's a miracle Juana Maria stayed alive all those years. Perhaps so. But the really miraculous thing to me is what survived inside her. Somehow, all the tragedy and loneliness in her life never diminished her capacity to be in a state of grace.

"She was as full of grace as anyone I've ever known. Juana Maria showed us all what I would call the better half of grace. Despite all the terrible events in her life, she was, as those who spent time around her can tell you, always cheerful, generous, and never angry about what happened to her.

"So, consider this question—could any of you here today endure what she did and act the same?

"As you know, the island from which she came was named after Saint Nicholas, who was known for giving gifts to those in need. And here, I believe, is a gift from the island which bears his name, one we can all share—the life of Juana Maria, who survived and overcame such loss and misfortune, so that we may all know the true capacity for courage and hope in the human spirit."

After Father Gonzalez finished, he introduced Pedro, who stepped forward to address the crowd.

"Most of you here today have never attended a funeral for an Indian. But today you are here, and I thank you for that.

"And now, to honor Juana Maria, I will sing her song for you."

We were not surprised when Pedro told us he had memorized Juana Maria's song and wanted to sing it at her funeral. Indians, for some reason, have an unusual ability to memorize the songs of others, even if they don't understand the meaning of the words. Since the time he first heard Juana Maria sing her song as she left San Nicolas, it was impressed into his memory. He also heard her sing it for the people who came to see her at my house.

As best as I can write it down, here are the words of Juana Maria's song that Pedro sang that day.

Tokitoki, yahami mina toki toki
Welelesh kima
Nishu yahami mina
Welelesh kima
Nishu yahami mina, tokotoki

Father Gonzalez ended the funeral with a prayer for the ascension of Juana Maria's soul. Then we lowered her coffin into the grave and the final procession began. Most everyone in Santa Barbara was there to say a final goodbye.

Afterwards, as we were about to leave, I saw Pedro having a conversation with a very old Indian man, and he motioned for Rosa and me to come over.

"This is Aravio," said Pedro, introducing the old man, "who is a Cruzeno Chumash now living in the Santa Ynez area."

Aravio was one of the oldest Indians I ever met. His face was deeply wrinkled and his body stooped over. I would guess he was about eighty years of age.

Pedro went on to explain that Aravio wanted to meet Juana Maria, but didn't get to Santa Barbara in time to do so.

"Over fifty years ago," Aravio said, "I was one of the last Indians living on Santa Cruz Island. As a young man I spent some time on San Nicolas and learned to speak the Nicoleño tongue. Even though it was so long ago, I thought I might remember enough to speak to Juana Maria."

It was hard to believe, but in a way it didn't surprise me—after all the bad luck suffered by Juana Maria, it figured that when we finally found someone who could possibly talk to her, it was too late.

Aravio then told us he was able to understand some of the words of Juana Maria's song. He wasn't sure, but thought they meant something like this—

> *I can go away, feeling contented*
> *Because I have seen the day*
> *When I leave this island*
> *To see my people again*

Rosa and I invited Zack, Pedro and Miguel and their families, Father Gonzalez and Aravio to our house for dinner that night. Before sitting down to eat, Rosa said there was something she wanted to say.

"I know it's a sad occasion, but to really honor Juana Maria we should put away our sadness and be happy—as she always was. We can also hope she's now at long last reunited with her people.

"I didn't know Juana Maria for very long, but I can say one thing about her that is certain—she never felt sorry for herself, and never wanted anyone else to. I believe she saw the world from a different perspective than the rest of us—a perspective that revealed only the good things in life and shut out everything else."

"I agree entirely," said Father Gonzalez. "Let's make an effort to not be sad tonight. I'll start by saying something that should give you all a pretty good laugh.

"As you know, Juana Maria was just a common Indian woman who couldn't even read or write, and never set foot in a house of Christian worship. But as we now know, she was the most extraordinary person we'll ever meet—someone who will always inspire us to survive whatever adversity may come our way.

"So," he said, while starting to laugh, "I can't help but be amused by the fact that the most inspirational person I ever met was someone with no education, who never read the Bible or worshipped our lord Jesus Christ."

"As you always like to say to us," joked Pedro, "God works in mysterious ways."

"Yes, and there are some mysteries we can never solve," said Zack. "Was it really God's intention for Juana Maria to be left behind on that island? For the *Peor es Nada* to sink?

For her to never see her people again? And for me to feel so guilty about what happened to her?

"In the end, I have to agree with Father Gonzalez—some things in life are a mystery. But one thing I know—despite all the guilt I have, I'll always feel blessed to have known her."

That night we received some interesting information from Aravio. He told us some things about San Nicolas Island and the Nicoleños that we would've never known otherwise. As best as I can remember, here is what he said:

"For as long as the people of my village could remember, there was trade and marriage between Santa Cruz Island and San Nicolas Island. My uncle and the wife of one my cousins were from San Nicolas, and several from our village married into the Nicoleño tribe.

"Our people regarded San Nicolas as the most special island of them all. This was because it is so far out into the ocean, and so distant from the other islands. To us it represented the boundary between this world and the next.

"A journey to San Nicolas was the most dangerous and challenging of all. When a canoe owner made that trip successfully it gave him great prestige and power. That is why, perhaps, the Indian name for that island is *Zalasat*, a word for the reward you receive when achieving some victory or great deed.

"I remember learning as a child that the Nicoleños made the most beautiful shell jewelry and figurines. However, San Nicolas Island did not have the wood needed to make canoe planks, so we often traded canoe planks for their jewelry and figurines.

"When the missions came, many of our people moved off the island, including some of those who knew how to make the canoes. So, one day the Nicoleños came to our island ready to trade, but we did not have any canoe planks.

"The Nicoleños were concerned about this, and asked if we would be able to continue making canoe planks for them. Our village chief promised them we would. To guarantee this, and in exchange for the items they'd brought to trade with us, he offered to send a young man from our village to San Nicolas with them. The young man he chose was me.

"And so that is how I came to spend time on San Nicolas Island, and why I could understand the song Pedro sang at the funeral. I was there for about six months, and it was a wonderful time for me. The Nicoleño people were different from the Cruzeno. They spoke a different language, and had a different way of living. They spent more time singing, storytelling and watching the night sky than did my people, and also were more skilled at making things such as baskets, jewelry, and figurines.

"I remember hearing that the Nicoleños originally came from a land to the south, and this was why they had a different language and way of living. But I do not know if that is really true or not. There were about a hundred Nicoleños on the island at that time, but in the past there were even more than that.

"One day two canoes from Santa Cruz arrived. They brought a large load of canoe planks for the Nicoleños. I remember my uncle telling them that the number of people on the other islands, including Santa Cruz, was decreasing. After hearing this, the chief of the Nicoleños insisted I return to my people.

"Soon after I returned to Santa Cruz, many people on the island became sick and died from the smallpox illness.

Eventually, those of us remaining decided to leave the island and move to the mainland, where I have been ever since.

"In my younger days I sometimes thought about the Nicoleños, and wondered what became of them. But over the years I stopped thinking about it, because I assumed they'd met the same fate as those on the other islands.

"A few weeks ago, someone in my village told me about the woman found on San Nicolas. At first I did not believe it, because I thought it was impossible any of the Nicoleños could've survived so long.

"A few days ago, I heard that the woman was thought to be the last of her tribe, and spoke a language no one could understand. It was then I realized she may be a Nicoleño after all, and so I decided to come to Santa Barbara. I'm very sorry I was too late.

"When I heard Pedro sing Juana Maria's song at the funeral, then I knew for sure she was a Nicoleño, because I could recognize some of the words.

"I will always regret coming too late to meet her. She was the last Nicoleño, who were a proud tribe and did not deserve such a fate. But I am happy she survived all those years, because now her story, and the story of her people, will never be forgotten."

A few years later, I suggested to Zack, Miguel and Pedro that we make another trip to San Nicolas for hunting, as it was getting harder to find otter around the other islands and the coastline. I was not too surprised that they did not want to go there again.

It was somewhat depressing, I will admit, to visit any of the Channel Islands. For countless years they were occupied by people who were now gone, with nothing but shell mounds to show they were even there.

"I do not wish to ever return to San Nicolas Island," said Pedro. "I would be thinking about Juana Maria and the Nicoleño people, and wondering if their spirits are still present there."

"I would prefer to remember the island by thinking of our last visit there," said Miguel. "It was a happy time. I will never forget the sound of Juana Maria's laughter as she played with the stuffed otter, or how beautiful the island looked in early spring. That is how we should all remember San Nicolas."

Over the years, Juana Maria became known as the Lone Woman of San Nicolas Island. Word of her story eventually spread to other places, and occasionally someone comes to Santa Barbara to talk to us about it.

There were a few articles written about it in newspapers and magazines, but nothing that ever really told the full story. For many years Zack, Pedro, Miguel, Father Gonzalez and Rosa and I planned to write down everything we knew about it, but somehow never got around to doing so.

Instead, we let the years pass by, always thinking there would be time to do it in the future. Then a few years ago Pedro and Miguel decided to move up to San Luis Obispo, to be closer to some of their children now living there.

Soon after that, Father Gonzalez suffered a stroke and passed away, after presiding over the Santa Barbara Mission church for forty years. His funeral was the biggest event in Santa Barbara since the funeral for Juana Maria.

About a year ago Rosa and I went to visit our son Jacob at his ranch on San Miguel Island. When we came back we got the sad news that Zack had taken ill with pneumonia and passed away. According to his wife Mary, just moments before dying, he asked her to pass on to me a last request—to tell this story.

In looking over what I have written down so far, I find there is still something yet to add. So the other night I took the time to sit down with Rosa and asked her to tell me her memories of this story. After all, she spent more time with Juana Maria than anyone else and, as she likes to remind me, it always helps to have a woman's perspective.

So, here are Rosa's recollections:

"I am an old woman now. Many years have passed since Juana Maria was here. But I remember that time very clearly, as clearly as I can recall anything that ever happened to me.

"I have much to thank God for. I came from a good family, married a good man and was blessed with four children. But it has been an ordinary life—except for the time Juana Maria was here. That was the most unusual and memorable event I ever experienced. In some ways it doesn't seem so long ago, because I still feel her presence in my life.

"My memories of Juana Maria begin many years before I actually met her. Back in 1835, I recall hearing the news about a woman left behind on San Nicolas Island. It touched me deeply and I couldn't stop thinking about it. I believed that somehow the woman would survive.

"After the sinking of the *Peor es Nada,* everyone around here forgot about her. I can't really explain why, but I continued to pray for her and think about her. I think Father Gonzalez was the only one besides me who did so.

"I remember talking to him about it. We were both disappointed that no other ship could be found after the *Peor es Nada* sank. We both believed someone was still alive out there.

"Even after Captain Whitmore searched the island, I could not stop thinking about it. For the next fifteen years I was haunted by the thought that someone was still living on San Nicolas.

"I was very relieved when the letter from Captain Whitmore came, because I knew my husband and Zack and the brothers would make a trip to San Nicolas. I would finally know the truth.

"When they returned and told me what they saw, I felt conflicting emotions. I was happy the woman was still alive, but disappointed she couldn't be found and that her fate was still uncertain.

"I began to worry about her future. If she came to Santa Barbara, would she adapt to her new life here? After so many years alone, would she be afraid of people, and unable to trust anyone? Could we find any of her people? Could she feel comfortable living with my family? Would she prefer to live with other Indians, even if they were not her tribe and spoke a different language? Would she miss San Nicolas Island and the way of life she had there?

"I thought about these questions all winter long. It was the longest winter of my life. I spent many hours praying for the woman to survive until George and the others returned in the spring.

"When *The Cora* set sail for San Nicolas the following May, the frequency of my prayers increased and the days got even longer. Finally, late in the afternoon one day, I spotted a ship on the horizon.

"I clearly remember the moment when *The Cora* got

close enough to shore to see Juana Maria on board. Despite my belief she could survive, when first seeing her I somehow couldn't believe my eyes.

"I felt a mix of emotions. Juana Maria had finally been rescued, but I worried if she could adapt to an entirely new world. I was also concerned because Father Gonzalez had been unable to find any of her people. I knew how disappointed she would be that no familiar faces were there to greet her.

"I was amazed when first observing Juana Maria up close as the ship approached the wharf. I thought she would be shy and withdrawn after being alone for so many years, but instead she was smiling and laughing and pointing at the things she'd never seen before. Father Gonzalez and I came forward and said a few words of welcome to her. She seemed to somehow understand what we said and smiled graciously and bowed to us.

"Juana Maria was delighted by all the children present on the wharf. She reached into one of her baskets, pulled out a number of knives made of bone, and gave one to each of the boys, then gave necklaces made of small pink shells to the girls. I soon realized that what made Juana Maria happiest was giving away whatever possessions she had, especially to children.

"As we walked off the wharf and onto the beach, Juana Maria met a horse and an ox for the first time, and surprised us by showing no fear of them at all. Instead, she approached the animals and wanted to touch them and examine them closely, and they did not shy away from her at all.

As she did this, George told Father Gonzalez and me how Juana Maria lost her child the day she got left behind.

He also explained how gracious and friendly she was when they first found her. It was then I began to realize what an extraordinary spirit had just entered our lives.

"The news about Juana Maria spread around town faster than a juicy bit of gossip. As we walked towards our house, dozens of people began following us in order to get a look at her. I knew by then that Juana Maria's arrival in Santa Barbara was going to be quite an event, maybe the biggest in the town's history. Everyone wanted to see her.

"That first day at our house was quite a scene. When Juana Maria put on her feather dress and sang and danced on our front veranda, about half the town was there to see it. I remember realizing that she'd seen more people that day than in her entire life up until then.

"What I really remember from that first night was something I alone witnessed. I decided to give Juana Maria a hot bath. I thought after such a long day she would like to clean herself. I also figured it would be a pleasurable experience for her, and something she never experienced on San Nicolas Island.

"When I first showed her the tub of hot water and made motions for her to get in, she seemed hesitant and began pointing at the tub and laughing and talking. I thought maybe she didn't understand I wanted her to undress and get in the tub, but then I realized she was just surprised we had gone to so much trouble and used so much water just for her to wash herself.

"After she finally got in, I gave her the soap and also a ladle we use for rinsing off. To show her how to use the soap, I rubbed a little on the side of her face. While doing so I saw her close her eyes, and a few seconds later she smiled. Then she took my hand in hers and held it to her face while continuing to smile.

"I realized she was simply enjoying the feeling of being physically touched. It's something we all take for granted, but Juana Maria went eighteen years without touching, or feeling the touch of, another human being.

"It was the most poignant moment of my life. I am usually not so emotional but in this case I could not help myself. My eyes began to water. When Juana Maria noticed a tear running down my face she stopped smiling and looked at me apologetically, as if to say she was sorry for making me cry. She then took the soap from my hand and began washing herself, and by the time she finished was once again smiling and talking away as usual.

"The next few days were busy for Juana Maria because so many people came to our house to see her. She continued to sing and dance in her feather dress and was always in good humor.

"I remember the day we took her to meet the Indians who came from the San Gabriel Mission. She was unable to communicate with any of them. It was certainly a terrible disappointment for her, and perhaps she was beginning to realize she might never see any of her people again. Even so, on the way back from the mission that day Juana Maria continued to be friendly to everyone who approached her.

"She was always looking for ways to be useful, and liked to help me with my daily chores. She was especially curious about cooking, and wanted to learn how I made bread and cooked meat and baked fruit pies.

"She was also eager to learn Spanish, and soon memorized my children's names and such words as *pan*, *papas*, *caballo* and *mañana*. She called George *tata* and called me *nana*.

"However, I gradually began to sense she was missing some things about her island life. So one day I took her for a long walk up and down the beach. She enjoyed this and went swimming in the ocean and collected many shells. She later used these shells to make more bracelets and necklaces, which she gave away to my children and others.

"I also wondered if she missed weaving baskets. George told me he saw her making baskets on the island, and the ones she brought with her were quite beautiful. So I took her to meet an old Indian woman in the village named Candaleria, who was considered the most skilled basket weaver in Santa Barbara. They became friends even though they couldn't speak to each other. Juana Maria always looked happy when weaving baskets with Candaleria and from that point on visited her almost every day.

"And so, after Juana Maria was here a while I had hope she would adapt to her new surroundings. However, I could sense how disappointed she was to not have seen any of her people.

"Soon after that, George and the others left for Los Angeles. They were gone about a week. I spent a lot of that time worrying about Juana Maria, knowing she would be heartbroken if their trip was unsuccessful.

"The day they returned marked a turning point for Juana Maria. The hope that sustained her for so many years started to die. Gradually, over the next few weeks she lost her will to live. Her walks on the beach and visits to Candaleria became less frequent until they stopped altogether. Her singing and dancing also stopped, and she lost interest in learning new Spanish words.

"She also began to lose her appetite. I thought that maybe a return to the food she ate at San Nicolas, such as seal and abalone, would help her. George procured such items for me and I cooked them and offered them to Juana Maria. She smiled and thanked me graciously but would not eat the food.

"I felt so helpless. Juana Maria had lost her will to live, and all we could do was hope she would somehow regain it. But we also knew she would never really feel at home here. We were not her people, could not speak her language, and lived a very different life from the one she lived on San Nicolas Island.

"Out there, she was the only person—it was just her, the island and the ocean. She must have felt the rhythms and cycles of nature in a way we can never know. Then suddenly she was living in a house and in a town with many other people around, and totally removed from the life she had on San Nicolas Island.

"As the Indian medicine woman Luisa explained to us, Juana Maria lived her whole life as a true Indian, and would not be able to live any other way. And when she found out her people were no longer present in this world, there was no reason for her to be here.

"Right up until the moment she died, Juana Maria was always smiling and thinking of others. The last thing she did before passing away was to take my hand, smile and point upwards. I think she wanted to tell me to not feel sad for her, because she was finally going to see her people. Despite all the suffering and loneliness in her life, she never expected anyone to feel sorry for her.

"So as hard as it may be, I try to never feel any sorrow when thinking about Juana Maria. Instead, I recall her ever-present smile, and imagine her long-awaited reunion with the other Nicoleños, in a place where no one is ever forgotten or alone."

With a little help from Rosa, I have fulfilled my friend Zack's dying wish and told the story of the Lone Woman of San Nicolas Island.

Of all the people involved in this story, Zack always felt the most guilt about it. He never forgave himself for the fateful decision made back in April of 1835—to keep on sailing to San Nicolas instead of turning around and waiting out that gale.

And yes, it's true that Zack's decision set off a series of events resulting in a woman being left alone for eighteen years. But as I often tried to tell him, what happened to Juana Maria was not just the result of one bad decision made by the impatient captain of a doomed ship.

I also don't believe you can place the blame solely on the Franciscan missionaries of the Catholic Church, or on the Russian hunters who brought the Kodiak Indians to San Nicolas Island. I see a less specific cause, which is the relentless determination of human beings to pursue our various desires, even when it means others may suffer. Whether the object of pursuit is an overseas empire, religious conversion, or merely the soft skins of the sea otter, the outcome, to varying degrees, is the same. I know this because throughout my life I've seen what happens when people put their mighty plans into motion without ever stopping to think of the consequences. The over-hunted otter and the beleaguered Indians, now largely gone from the California landscape, are just two examples of this.

And so the story of a lone woman on a distant island is not merely an isolated episode of early California history. It is also a timeless fable that makes us ponder our past mistakes and consider how we might do things differently in the future.

Although many years have passed since Juana Maria's death, Rosa and I still think about her often. We wonder if the world will ever again see such a stark example of the limitless endurance a woman can summon when she has something to live for, and how quickly her spirit will die when she doesn't. The mere hope of seeing her people again provided all the spiritual sustenance Juana Maria needed to survive the loss of her child and eighteen years of unbroken solitude. But when that hope disappeared she was gone within a few weeks.

And yet we don't consider Juana Maria's story a purely sad one, perhaps because of the joy and laughter she graced us with during her time here. We also know her story will continue to be told for as long as stories are told, and always find a place in the hearts of those who hear it. In particular, whoever has suffered from some cruel twist of fate, we hope this story will inspire you to overcome it, and do so, as Juana Maria did, with a joyous and generous spirit.

As for me, well, if for nothing else I will at least be remembered for my role in finding the heroine of this extraordinary story. The way I look at it, though, is that while I did help find Juana Maria, in a way she also helped find me.

You see, her presence in my life brought me to the end of a long journey. It was a journey at first marked by vengeful anger and blind ignorance. But then that mysterious thing called fate led me to the lovely little pueblo of Santa Barbara, where I crossed paths with a Chumash Indian who saved my life, and a Nicoleño woman who showed me how to live it. Thanks to them, I finally came to know the truth about the people I once considered my enemy, and the world we both live in. As Rosa likes to remind me, I've still got my share of faults, but at least this old man is full of hope, without complaint, and keenly aware of the need for forgiveness and redemption.

Rosa and I occasionally visit the mission cemetery to say a prayer for the departed soul of the person we called Juana Maria, whose true name was never learned, but will forever be remembered by history as the Lone Woman of San Nicolas Island.

— The End —

Author's Note

This novel is based on a true story. There really was a Lone Woman of San Nicolas Island, who was left behind there in 1835 and survived eighteen years before finally being found in 1853.

There also was a man named George Nidever (the brother of my great, great grandfather), who found the Lone Woman and whose family she lived with after leaving San Nicolas.

However, this novel is a blend of fact and fiction, with a fair dose of "historical liberty" added in. It could not be otherwise, due to the paucity of in-depth, first-hand accounts of this singular episode of early California history. This is why, despite the considerable interest shown in this story over the years since it took place, no one has ever published a full-length, nonfiction book about the Lone Woman's life. There is simply not nearly enough recorded or documented information to make such a book possible.

There are only two firsthand accounts of the story, neither one of which is very lengthy. In 1878, a researcher from the University of California came to Santa Barbara and induced George Nidever to tell his life story, which was eventually published in 1937 with the title *The Life and Adventures of George Nidever*. This book is just eighty-nine pages, and the section of it recounting the story of the Lone

Woman is only twelve pages.

The other first-hand account is by a man named Carl Dittman, who was actually with Nidever when the Lone Woman was finally found (this book blends Dittman and Isaac Sparks into one character). The same researcher who interviewed Nidever also interviewed Dittman, and his recollections were published under the title *Narrative of a Seafaring Life on the Coast of California*. Dittman's account of the Lone Woman story is quite similar to Nidever's. Both accounts are frustratingly short and leave many unanswered questions.

In addition to these accounts, a magazine article about the Lone Woman was published in 1880 by *Scribner's Monthly*. It was written by Emma Hardacre and is titled "18 Years Alone." Hardacre apparently interviewed George Nidever (who lived until 1883) and others familiar with the story, and her version of it is about fifteen pages in length. However, for various reasons I doubt the veracity of parts of this article, and it is certainly not a definitive or comprehensive version of the Lone Woman story.

For those interested in reading everything that was recorded about this story, I recommend getting a copy of the University of California Archeological Survey #55, titled *Original Accounts of the Lone Woman of San Nicolas Island,* edited by UC archeologists Robert F. Heizer and Albert B. Elsasser, and published in 1961. This includes the aforementioned recollections of Nidever and Dittman, the Emma Hardacre article, and other shorter pieces pertaining to the Lone Woman story.

If interested in a more thorough look of what happened to California Indians during the Spanish/Mexican/American invasion of this state, I recommend the book *The Other*

AUTHOR'S NOTE

Californians, by Robert Heizer and Alan Almquist, published in 1971 by University of California Press. It was in this book I found details of the massacre of women and children by the vigilante group, and the execution of the Indian converts.

Subsequent to the publication of the above, anthropologist Travis Hudson discovered further information about the Lone Woman. This can be found in the *Journal of California and Great Basin Anthropology*, Vol. 3, No. 2, 1981, and is titled "Recently Discovered Accounts Concerning the Lone Woman of San Nicolas Island." This article provided the lyrics and translation of the Lone Woman's song.

In 1997, a photo book titled *Native Americans on the Central Coast* was published by the Black Gold Cooperative Library System in Ventura, California. This book includes an old photo of an Indian woman said to be a "possible portrait" of the Lone Woman (you can see the photo on the Wikipedia page for Juana Maria). My research strongly suggests this photo is not one of Juana Maria, but there is no way to definitely prove this.

To interested readers I recommend the novel *Island of the Blue Dolphins*, published in 1960 and written by award-winning author Scott O'Dell. You may remember reading this in school, and although classified as juvenile fiction, it is a book that can be enjoyed by all ages.

Though based on the same true story, *Island of the Blue Dolphins* differs from this book in several ways. It is almost entirely fictional, whereas this book draws heavily on the recollections of Nidever and Dittman and provides a historical context for the story. The narrator in *Island of the Blue Dolphins* is the Lone Woman herself. The whole novel takes place on San Nicolas, and ends when she is rescued.

Therefore, even though both novels are based on the same story, they are quite different (or, you might say, they complement each other). *Finding the Lone Woman of San Nicolas Island* is the first novel to attempt a complete version of this story.

One thing in particular I tried to keep as close as possible to Nidever and Dittman's recollections was my depiction of the character and personality of the Lone Woman.

For example, from Dittman's account we have the following descriptions of her first response to being found, etc.:

"I stepped around in front of her, but instead of being startled and alarmed, I was surprised to have her bow and smile, as though it was a delight to see me and my visit an everyday occurrence. She began a rapid talking and gesticulating. As fast as the men approached her she also bowed, smiled and talked to them. Taking some roots from two bags or sacks made of grass she placed them in the coals and as soon as they were roasted she passed them around making motions for us to eat."

"She was always anxious to help when she saw an opportunity of making herself useful. She was always cheerful and always talking and laughing. ..."

"Visitors made her presents of trinkets and sometimes of money but she placed no value on one or the other unless it be the pleasure she felt in dividing them among the children of Nidever's family."

Dittman and Nidever also recounted the scene of the stuffed otter, the stopping of the wind while on the way from San Nicolas to Santa Barbara, and the Lone Woman's delight upon seeing an ox and a horse for the first time. Nidever also said the following about her:

AUTHOR'S NOTE

"She was always in good humor and sang and danced, to the great delight of the children and even older ones."

Due to these and other statements, I believe that the depiction in this book of the character and personality of the Lone Woman is quite believable.

The offers by the two ship captains to "buy" the Lone Woman is also true. It is testimony to how captivated people were by Juana Maria's story, and also how Indians were treated in those days. Fortunately, Nidever and his family "had all become somewhat attached to her, and consequently refused to listen to these proposals."

Juana Maria's belongings, such as her water baskets, bone needles, etc. were sent to the California Academy of Sciences in San Francisco, and destroyed in the 1906 earthquake/fire. Her feather dress was apparently sent to the Vatican, but it never arrived or was lost. The only known surviving artifacts are an abalone shell fishhook, an arrowhead and a stone weapon of some kind, which are held privately in Santa Barbara.

At some point over the years, her grave was moved and now cannot be located. A memorial plaque was placed in the mission cemetery in 1928.

Father Junipero Serra was recently canonized by the Catholic Church. Not surprisingly, this action was opposed by California Indian tribes, who have started a campaign to have the canonization rescinded.

Archeological work on San Nicolas over the years indicates that the island was inhabited for at least four thousand years, and at times may have had a population exceeding one thousand people.

Today, San Nicolas Island is occupied by the U.S. Navy, which is allowing further archeological work to be done there, so perhaps in the future we will learn more about the long-ago vanished tribe who used to call it home and the woman whose life inspired this book.

Acknowledgments

A huge "thank you" goes to all of my friends and family members whose input and moral support helped me write this book, especially Anita Clark, Thelda Eli, Glenda Southard, Bruce Lawrence, Judi Loren Grace, Cheryl Symmes, Yumi Tsukumi, and R. J. and Syan Nidever.

Thanks also to my dogs Toby and Buster for keeping me in good health by their daily insistence on a walk through the woods.

Extra-special thanks go to my mom, Hedley Cooper, and my wife, Kayoko Nakano. Without their support and encouragement this book would not have been.

About the Author

R.C. Nidever was born in Sacramento, California. He attended American River College and the University of California, Los Angeles, is a former journalist and magazine editor, and lives in a small northern California town.

For more information about this book and the author, please visit www.rcnidever.com or email rcnidever@gmail.com.

www.ingramcontent.com/pod-product-compliance
Lightning Source LLC
LaVergne TN
LVHW051833080426
835512LV00018B/2843